OWNING IT

Proven Strategies for Success in ALL of Your Roles as a Teacher Today

By Alex Kajitani
CALIFORNIA TEACHER OF THE YEAR

D0391730

Edited by Megan Pincus Kajitani

• SECOND EDITION •

eaRLY PRaISe FOR
OWNING IT

Named "Recommended Reading" by the United States Department of Education.

"No jargon. No fads. Instead every page has so much you can use immediately, at no cost, to enhance your success as a teacher. Buy this book as soon as possible."

> ------ Harry and Rosemary Wong,
> Authors of the Bestselling Book,
> *The First Days of School*

"Alex Kajitani gives expert advice 'from the trenches' in an easy style that feels like a chat with a trusted colleague over coffee. There is something for everyone (teacher or administrator) wishing to improve their practice and lead their school to positive change."

> ------ Kim Reed, Principal, Conway Elementary
> School, Escondido, CA

"It's tough being a teacher in urban schools. In a field where so many voices are critical, argumentative and/or defensive, along comes a sane and thoughtful compendium of practical suggestions.

Alex Kajitani has crafted techniques, large and small, which can provide immediate help to all teachers — newcomers or veterans — who want more for themselves and their students.

This book is a veritable Swiss Army knife of ideas for meeting the daily challenges of daily instruction. It is a huge contribution to improving the lives of teachers and students in America. There is nothing quite like it in our field."

> ------ Robert W. Blackburn, Ph.D., Professor
> of Educational Leadership, California
> State University-East Bay and Former
> Superintendent of Oakland Public Schools

"One of the hallmarks of a great teacher is the commitment to being a lifelong learner. In *Owning It*, Alex Kajitani demonstrates this commitment and eloquently shares the valuable lessons he has learned along the way.

The 25 practical essays in this book contain the pearls of wisdom that Alex has collected over his years in the classroom, his work with at-risk students, his interactions with colleagues and his involvement in the community. Each insightful essay provides information in a clear and fresh manner.

This is a book I wish I had years ago when I started teaching. Now it is one that I want to make sure is in the hands of my colleagues so that collectively, for the good of all of our students, we will begin to *own it*."

— Beth Ekre, North Dakota Teacher of the Year

"I have been working with new teachers for over 15 years now, and I've seen so many of them struggle to work well with their new school communities. This book is a perfect toolkit for success in so many dimensions of this work.

I love how Alex Kajitani lays out such specific approaches to integrate, support and collaborate inside and outside of the school building.

Read this book and strengthen your approach to a new school workplace — and likely also strengthen the entire teaching profession. Own it!"

— Zachary Perin, Ed.M., Senior Managing Director, Teach For America

"As a former teacher and coach, I understand the necessity of teamwork to be successful in school, business, and life. As the current superintendent for a dropout recovery public charter high school, I believe that we need all the resources we can get to guide us in making the right decisions for our students, and ultimately, the community.

Owning It is a motivational book that gives fresh new insight and easy-to-implement strategies for the important work we do for our students."

— Linda C. Dawson, Ed.D., SIATech Superintendent/CEO and Board President & Co-Founder, Reaching At-Promise Students Association (RAPSA)

For my wonderful wife, Megan. Each time you edit my words, you change the trajectory of what I realize is possible in this world.

— A.K.

A Kajitani Education publication— *Educating for the world as it can be.*

Book Design by Bamboo Star Studios
with Jeff Pincus and Angel Printing, Oceanside, California

Author photograph by Earnie Grafton, *San Diego Union-Tribune*

contents

OWNING IT. ... IN YOUR CLASSROOM

PART ONE: TEACHER AS CLASSROOM LEADER

Section 1: *Strategies for Creating an Environment
of Achievement*

Section 2: *Special Strategies for Succeeding With At-Risk and Struggling Students and Populations*

OWNING IT... AT YOUR SCHOOL

PART TWO: TEACHER AS COLLEAGUE

OWNING IT... THROUGHOUT THE COMMUNITY

PART THREE: TEACHER AS PUBLIC PROFESSIONAL

INTRODUCTION

There's this myth in teaching. This myth that says you will struggle in your first few years but that, by your fourth or fifth year, you'll be experienced, things will be easy and you'll have your act together.

The truth is that while some years are better than others, teaching is hard *every* year. And every year, as teachers, we are asked to do more and more.

We live in a time of what some theorists call "accelerating change" — with exponentially faster technological, cultural, social and environmental change than any other period in the known history of our planet. And we're feeling this firsthand in our schools, and in our profession.

Each year, the group of students that enters our classrooms is vastly different from the group a year before. They are deeply influenced by the latest technology, the year's hit television (or Internet) show, and new ways of thinking and operating in society.

And yet, as teachers, it is still our responsibility to ensure that they learn the academic content that someone else has deemed they learn, along with non-curricular life skills.

As teachers, it is also our responsibility to work with one another to help these kids learn — which means we have to master grown-up communication and collaboration skills.

And, as teachers, it's our responsibility to represent our profession — and our schools and districts, and even our nation's educational system — to the wider community, the "public," via all of the ever-changing modes of communication.

Being a teacher today is a multi-skill, multi-faceted, multi-purpose role — a role that doesn't end when the bell rings, rather one we embody in our classrooms, in our schools and throughout our communities.

Thus the great, challenging, overwhelming, enlightening and rewarding responsibility it is: *to be a teacher today.*

Let's *own* this great challenge, and great responsibility — and great *opportunity* to make a difference — that is being a modern-day teacher.

WHαT THIS BOOK IS

Seven years ago, I gave a presentation at a national conference for the non-profit organization, Reaching At-Promise Students Association (RAPSA).

My presentation — called "Making Math Cool" — was about strategies I was using in my urban middle school math classroom to engage students and help them connect math to their real lives. I also talked about my then-recently-released CD, *The Rappin' Mathematician*, of math-related rap songs I'd recorded after they were a hit in my classroom, and other colleagues' classrooms as well.

Little did I know that I was about to hit a pivotal turning point in my teaching career. At that conference, I first met Dr. Harry K. Wong, author of the classic book on classroom management, *The First Days of School*, and he later became one of my mentors (beyond his book, which had been a mentor to me itself).

And, after that conference, the director of RAPSA asked me if I would write a bi-monthly teaching column for their national newsletter, to which I happily agreed.

Soon after that conference, my *Rappin' Mathematician* CD (which became two CDs and an activity book) began to catch on with teachers and parents across the country. I began getting recognized for my work inside and outside of the classroom, winning awards such as Middle School Math Teacher of the Year for Greater San Diego, as well as getting invited to present at more conferences around the nation.

Three years after the RAPSA conference, I was selected as a San Diego County Teacher of the Year, then in a whirlwind period that followed, the California Teacher of the Year, and then a Top-4 Finalist for National Teacher of the Year. This ride took me to the White House on President Obama's 99th day in office, and it landed me on many a radio and TV news show, including *The CBS News with Katie Couric.*

This also happened to be a time in my personal life when I had a toddler daughter and, a month before I flew cross-country to the White House ceremony, a newborn son. All the while, I stayed committed to my classes of at-risk students — in one of California's most poverty-stricken neighborhoods — who needed me to teach them each day in Room 12 of the middle school where I worked.

And, all the while, I kept writing my bi-monthly columns for RAPSA about what I was experiencing and learning about being a modern-day teacher on the frontlines. While my audience for these columns was RAPSA members — teachers who worked at low-performing schools and/or with at-risk students — many of the topics I wrote about were universal to all classroom teachers.

I didn't have a grand plan when writing these columns. I just sat down every other month and wrote about what I was experiencing in my classroom, and later, when I became a coach for teachers in my school district, in my work with individual and teams of teachers.

Two things I did *always* focus on when writing my columns, however, were:

1) offering teachers *concrete, easy-to-implement strategies* on whatever topic I was discussing — strategies they could use *immediately* after reading each month's column, and

2) being both *real* about our roles as teachers, and also *inspirational* about "owning" the important work we do, because both are a core part of who I am as a teacher and a teacher-coach.

Seven years after becoming a columnist for RAPSA, I sat down and looked through all of the columns I'd written, and realized that, as a collection, they provide something I'm now working to share with teachers around the country as a "teacher of teachers."

These columns offer both an exploration of our many roles as teachers today, and a quick-reference handbook of strategies that can be pulled out in many of the range of situations we find ourselves in daily in our classrooms, schools and communities.

So, the RAPSA leadership team and I sat down and decided it was time to turn my columns into a book for teachers. A book that will help teachers feel more prepared for our multi-faceted roles today, and a book that will inspire teachers — like you — to remember why you entered this greatest profession, and what incredibly important work you do every day.

That's what this book is. It's a collection of 25 of what I chose as the most relevant of my columns over the past seven years. It's a book of strategies and inspiration.

It's a book about "owning it" — stepping up to and claiming our myriad roles as a modern teacher, and acing each one — for the benefit of our students, our schools, our communities, our profession, and even our nation.

And it's a book I hope *any teacher* can pick up and find something useful to implement in your work and life *right away*, along with some validation about how amazing you are, juggling all of the roles we teachers fill in today's fast-changing era.

HOW THIS BOOK IS STRUCTURED

Lots of teaching books focus on our role in the classroom, and so does this one. But, this book does something else I've not found in the many teaching books I read: it *also* focuses on our role in our school, as a colleague and member of a staff team; *and* on our role as a public professional, representing our profession throughout the wider community.

So, I divided this book into three parts, one focusing on each of these roles — our role as Classroom Leader, Colleague, and Public Professional. Excelling in all of these roles is critical at this time in our profession, and it is what's needed to be an excellent teacher in today's environment.

PART ONE: TEACHERS AS CLASSROOM LEADERS

Each year in the classroom, I had students in my class, who, despite living in dire poverty, performed at the top of the chart on state tests. Sitting next to them were students who could not read, tell time, or speak English. Yet I was expected to teach them all, at a level that was challenging to each of them.

That's why Part One of this book is devoted to the role we play, not as teachers of a specific subject or level, but as *teachers of kids*. As *classroom leaders* who are responsible for every kind of everyday learning, who are accountable to test scores and parents, and to every child who crosses our doorway.

Over seven years, I penned a lot of columns on this foundational role we play as classroom teachers, so I divided Part One into two sections:

Part One, Section 1 provides easy-to-implement, specific strategies that *all teachers* can use to connect with, engage, and ensure learning for all students.

In this section, I share what I learned on the ground in my classroom about such topics as how to increase our powerful presence in the classroom, how to use the first five minutes of class to set the tone, how to engage and encourage all students, and how to manage such realities of classroom teaching today as standardized tests and data.

This section can be a quick-reference guide for any teacher looking for a little burst of fresh air in their day-to-day teaching, or for ways to handle the challenging classroom situations all teachers face.

Part One, Section 2 focuses on the 20% of our collective students that provide 80% of our challenges in the classroom (and for some of us who teach in low-performing schools, this 20% makes up almost all of our students).

They are the students who are most challenging to connect with, to keep on task, and to help perform academically. They are the students who frustrate us, often to the point of exasperation.

They are also the students who need us the most. They are the students whose parents may not be deeply committed to their education or were, themselves, unsuccessful in school. They're the students who fall into the "achievement gap," and often are lost in there.

That's why the second section of Part One is devoted specifically to the ever-important role we play as teachers of at-risk and struggling students. In this section, I offer strategies on topics such as connecting with at-risk students, negotiating with them, honoring their cultural backgrounds, involving their sometimes discouragingly uninvolved parents, and empowering them to have a stake in their own education.

PART TWO: Teachers as Colleagues

The days of the one-room, one-teacher schoolhouse are long gone, and today working with a group of colleagues is an essential part of being a teacher. Just as we teach a group of students with a wide range of abilities and experiences, the teachers and administrators we work with are vastly different in their experiences, knowledge and philosophies.

We're not all teachers for the same reason, yet we're all expected to do the same job. And with 50% of our colleagues leaving this job within the first five years, the time has come for all of us to *own* the fact that as educators, we are truly interdependent upon each other.

That's why Part Two of this book is devoted to the role we play as colleagues — both in our schools and within our districts or organizations. It provides practical and real strategies that can be used to *incorporate, not eliminate* our differences, and draw upon each other's strengths.

Offering strategies ranging from creative ideas for staff meetings, to addressing the generation gaps (yes, gaps!) and new teachers on our school staffs today, to how to approach a colleague to have a difficult conversation, to how to create successful professional development events and job-shares, this section is based on the belief that the *number one factor in the success or failure of a school is the relationships of the adults in the building.*

PART THREE: TEACHERS AS PUBLIC PROFESSIONALS

Teaching is not just what we do. Teaching is what we are. It doesn't end when the last bell rings, or when vacation starts.

As a profession, we're constantly under attack from lawmakers, parent groups and the general public who have bought into the idea that our education system is failing, and that the solution is to simply "fire all the bad teachers."

So, the final section of this book is devoted to the role that we play as public professionals, representing our schools, our students and the whole convoluted concept of education today. The time has come to *own* this role, too.

The strategies I offer in Part Three include how to positively represent our schools and our profession in the public eye, how to utilize mass communication mediums to do so, how to step up and become a teacher leader, and how to help combat myths that hold our students back (well, at least one particular myth that is near and dear to my heart).

HOW TO USE THIS BOOK

You don't need to read this book from cover to cover (although I hope you will). It's meant to be read easily and efficiently, and every strategy is designed to be immediately implementable with little to no cost to you.

You can leave this book near your desk or nightstand and pull it out to read just one column on an issue you're dealing with at the moment, or to get a little jolt of motivation on a hard day. I also hope you will consider reading it as a group with your school or district staff teams, and working on the strategies together.

In the end, use this book however it works for you, to inspire yourself to "own it" — *own* your complex and expanding role, in the most important profession, in the most rapidly-changing time in history.

Let's "own it" together, and show the world that the future of education is brighter than some may think, with teachers like us taking the lead in our classrooms, our schools and our communities.

PART ONE

TEACHER AS CLASSROOM LEADER

Part One, Section 1:
Strategies for Creating an
Environment of Achievement

1

Time to Get Real

Revisiting the Value of a Personal Teaching Philosophy

Allow me to take you back to the days when you were training to become a teacher. For some, that time was many years ago; for others, it really was just yesterday.

In my credential program, our first assignment was a two-page essay on our "Philosophy of Teaching." A year later, at the end of the program, our director told us that the first question a job interviewer would ask us would be, "What is your philosophy of teaching?"

While I wasn't actually asked that question in my interviews, I always saw the importance of the question, for teachers new and seasoned. It makes us think about what we do and why, and it holds us accountable.

Over a decade later, having worked with countless students and having experienced all of the challenges, rewards, thinking and rethinking that are associated with teaching, I have finally pieced together enough information to truly answer that first important question. And my philosophy can be summarized in two words: *be real.*

I want to share this philosophy with you here, as a motivation to start off a new teaching year or semester, as a reminder for myself, and as a call to reconsider (or consider for the first time) your own teaching philosophy in action. Feel free to use my philosophy as you see fit — as fellow teachers in the trenches, I think it will resonate with you.

WHAT MY PHILOSOPHY MEANS

Be real means be real with yourself, and be real with your students. Teaching is an art, a science, a passion, and an opportunity. It is an opportunity to prepare our students not only for the world as it is, but for the world *as it can be*. It's an opportunity to summon the past, to examine the present, and to shape the future.

True teaching takes courage. It takes persistence. It takes honest self-reflection in order to continuously improve. It requires being real with oneself about what is necessary to be a great teacher.

In my philosophy of teaching, there are three main aspects of being real:

1. **Teach what is real.** No subject, especially the mathematics that I teach, can be truly learned if the students do not see the relevance of the information in their everyday lives. I am constantly looking for ways to "meet them where they live." On any given day, I am weaving lessons about the math the students are learning with issues important to them, such as advertising, the Internet, and popular music. Never will a student leave my class thinking that they will not use the information we have discussed.

2. **Be reliable.** My students know what is expected of them well before they enter my classroom each day. My expectations of them, the procedures in my classroom, and my relaxed, yet firm and consistent, manner are all aspects of my teaching that my students can rely on. As I embody the traits of a reliable human being, my students learn what it takes to be a reliable human being. We cannot demand that our students be organized, focused, and passionate unless we ourselves are all of these.

3. **Be realistic.** Teaching in one of San Diego's poorest neighborhoods, my students are constantly dealing with serious issues of violence, racism, and low literacy rates (to name just a few). It is not realistic that each one of my

students will show up on the first day proficient in their academic content areas. However, throughout the year, I take students from where they are to where they can be.

I believe that every student in my class can learn, can improve, and can surpass any expectations of themselves — regardless of where those expectations previously began and ended. Perhaps not every one of my students will graduate from college; however, each and every one of them will someday be a neighbor, a co-worker, and someone who has the potential to make a better world for those who come after them.

OWNING YOUR PHILOSOPHY

Educating is hard, and these times are hard. Educating at-risk and struggling students is arguably the hardest job there is. However, I truly believe that, as teachers, we are working for those with the most potential to create a brighter future for everyone. This is why I teach, and this is why I love teaching. It is the opportunity for real teaching, and teaching what is real.

When you next enter your classroom, ask yourself: *what is my own teaching philosophy? Am I owning it? What more can I do to put it into action?* Your teaching, and your students, will benefit from you asking these important questions. Whether or not you've ever answered the "teaching philosophy question" before, you can answer it now, and hold yourself to your answer.

Here's to getting real, and getting to the heart of being teachers.

2

VISIBILITY IS eVeRYTHING

HOW TO InCReaSe YOUR POWeRFUL PReSence In THe CLaSSROOM *(OR: HOW a BROKen WInDOW CHanGeD mY TeaCHInG FOReVeR)

As a new teacher, I really struggled. All the typical "new teacher" clichés applied: students constantly off-task, I shouted more "be quiet or else" warnings than I had time to enforce, and I left school each day feeling disrespected and, above all, that my students hadn't learned anything that day. I'd excelled in all of my teaching theory classes in my credential program, and had been a pretty decent student teacher. But now, on my own in a real classroom, I was sinking.

Then one day, my dad gave me a book that had seemingly nothing to do with teaching. And yet, it changed my teaching forever. *The Tipping Point,* by Malcolm Gladwell, outlined the work of two sociologists, James Wilson and George Kelling, and their "Broken Windows Theory."

THe BROKen WInDOWS THeORY

The Broken Windows Theory is quite simple. It's based on the belief that crime is the *inevitable result of disorder.*

Thus, if you walk by a building with a broken window (or several), you make the connection in your mind that *nobody cares for that building,* and that if you choose, you are free to go into the building and commit more (and more severe) crimes, with very little

23

potential for punishment. Gladwell paints the picture of New York City in 1990, when crime was at an all-time high, and 20,000 felonies per year were being committed on the subway system alone.

Believing that the city's history of letting seemingly small, insignificant crimes go unpunished for many years had created in peoples' minds the perception that they were free to commit more serious crimes, the mayor and police chief decided to implement the Broken Windows Theory. They ordered the police to crack down on two of the city's most visible crimes: graffiti and subway turnstile jumping.

Though they received much criticism for putting so much energy and resources into the "small criminals," by 1996, felonies in New York City had fallen by 75%, and murders dropped by 66%. Public perception changed from one of chaos to orderliness, and the health and productivity of the city was restored.

APPLYING THIS THEORY TO THE CLASSROOM

And that's when it occurred to me: if the Broken Windows Theory could turn around one of the world's largest cities, could it turn around my classroom as well?

The next morning, I walked into my classroom, determined to change public (my students') perception of my classroom. I decided to crack down on the two most "visible crimes": chewing gum and arriving late to class. I announced to my classes that chewing gum or walking in late to class would result in an automatic detention, and I cracked down hard.

I devoted all my energy that day to "catching" those committing these two "minor" offenses. It was exhausting. The next day, I devoted about 50% of my time toward this, and the next, just a little. By the end of the week, my students were on-task, following directions, and dare I say, learning. The following week, when I announced that I would be gone one day and that a substitute

24

teacher would be taking my place, I overheard a student say, "I'm not misbehaving when the sub is here. Mr. Kajitani will bust you for gum — *just imagine* what he'll do if you act out for a sub!"

It was at that point that I realized: **Visibility is Everything.** When it comes to classroom management, our students' perception of what is happening in our classrooms determines how they act while in
our classrooms.

FIVE STRATEGIES TO "SEE ALL" IN YOUR CLASSROOM (AND BEYOND)

These five tips can help you increase your powerful presence in the classroom, while keeping your students focused on the learning at hand:

1. **Make phone calls home.** Before the first day of school starts, I call the home of every one of my students (yeah, it takes a while, but the time I save not dealing with discipline issues throughout the year comes back ten-fold). I ask to speak with the students themselves, and I firmly tell them that I will be their (math) teacher this year, that they need to be in their seat in Room 12 before the bell rings, that they need to have a pencil and paper each day, and that chewing gum is absolutely prohibited. Before they even set foot on campus, I have created the perception that I am strict, organized and in control.

2. **Honk and wave while driving to school.** As I drive through the neighborhood in which my school is located each morning, I often see my students walking along the sidewalks. I always honk and wave to them as I drive past. Not too excitedly, but just enough to send them the message that my classroom extends far beyond its walls, and I'm looking out for them at all times. Would-be "ditchers" always have to reconsider, as they know I've already seen them, and will expect them in my class. As I

walk onto campus, I always say a pleasant "Good Morning" to every student I walk by, just to remind them that I see them, wherever they are.

One of my best friends is a successful real estate developer. He makes it a point to attend every networking event in the area. He says, "The reason I go is not just to meet new people, but I want everyone in the business to know that if they cheat me on a commission, they're going to have to see me everywhere they go." Needless to say, very few people have ever tried to take advantage of him. We send the same message to our students every time we greet them outside of our classrooms.

3. **Greet your students at the door.** Nothing says "I'm in control" more than your initial contact with your students as they enter your classroom. As you greet them, insist on eye contact as well. This can be a tough challenge, especially in cultures where eye contact is considered disrespectful, particularly with authority figures. Take the time to speak with your students about the importance of eye contact in our culture. Practice it, insist on it, and enjoy its benefits. Visibility works both ways.

4. **Utilize the eyes in the back of your head.** One of my absolute favorite classroom management tricks goes something like this:

   • You see that two of your students (we'll call them Jen and Ben) are off-task across the room. Instead of immediately correcting them, *remain silent.*

   • Walk to the opposite side of the room, and begin helping another student. With your back completely turned, say loudly, "Jen and Ben, please stop talking and finish your work." Never look up or make eye contact with Jen or Ben. Continue helping the original student.

- Jen and Ben will be shocked, and will wonder how you knew they were talking.

Again, you've created the perception that you are everywhere all at once, and affirmed that as teachers, visibility is everything. This trick works while you are working at the board, or sitting at your desk. Each time, continue about your business as if it's a regular part of your teaching. Of course, use your best judgment when dealing with more severe cases of discipline.

5. **Insist on a clean floor.** One minute before class ends, I announce to my students, "This floor was spotless when you walked in; it needs to be spotless as you walk out." I train the students to pick up any trash around the vicinity of their desk, whether or not they are responsible for it being there. Again, this helps maintain the impression that everything that is happening in my classroom is visible, and that everyone in the classroom is accountable. It also sets up the next class to be successful as students enter.

Just as the Broken Windows Theory cleaned up New York City, it can restore and promote order to your classroom as well. You just have to be willing to crack down hard on the most visible offenses in your classroom. What are they? Name them, crack down hard on them, and get back to teaching those students who need you.

3

FIRST IMPRESSIONS

MAKING THE MOST OF THE CRITICAL FIRST FIVE MINUTES OF ANY CLASS

Remember the old Head & Shoulders shampoo tagline? *You never get a second chance to make a first impression.*

As teachers, we actually get a chance to make a first impression *every single day* — often several times per day with each class we teach. And with today's students, who are accustomed to the rapidly-paced sound bytes and topic switches of a new media world, if we don't grab their attention quickly, we know that they often tune us out and the rest of the class is usually shot.

That's why the first five minutes of any class is so crucial: it is an opportunity to connect with our students, set the tone, convey our expectations, and state, in clear terms, why the class is even happening at all.

Before I was a teacher, I managed a seafood restaurant on the California coast. There, I learned many valuable lessons about the impact of first impressions. And while our students can't easily walk out and choose another place to go to school if we don't quickly meet their needs for connection, engagement, quality and comfort (as restaurant customers are apt to do), our students can certainly choose to not participate if those needs are not met — and then everyone loses.

Here are five critical steps — from this former restaurant manager-turned teacher — toward making the first five minutes of your class both efficient and effective:

1. **Connect quickly.** Ever walked into a restaurant and stood inside the door with a blank look on your face, waiting for the host or hostess to come and greet you — but the staff just whizzes around you, not acknowledging that you're there? Think about the stark contrast of this to the restaurant where someone greets you promptly at the door, warmly welcomes you, and has water and bread at the table as you're getting comfortable.

    Perhaps warm bread isn't a part of our pedagogy, but good customer service should be. When we greet and acknowledge our students as they enter our classrooms, we make them feel welcome, relaxed and happier to be there. Obviously, there are times when greeting each student by name is not possible; however eye contact, an affirming head nod or a thumbs-up is often enough connection for our students to feel noticed and welcome. This means they are also more open to learning. In addition, it firmly sets the tone that, as the teacher, you are well-prepared, in charge, and happy to be there.

2. **Lose the lull.** Continuing with the restaurant analogy, when the tables are full and a wait is required, what do smart restaurants have us do? *Preview the menu.* Read the daily specials, think about the foods ahead of us. This keeps us from getting bored and irritated, gives us time to process and ask questions, and eliminates confusion. By the time we are seated at a table, we are usually hungry, decisive, and ready to order.

    As our students sit down at their desks, they should never have to ask "Now, what?" On the very first day of school,

I train my students that each day they enter, a warm-up will be displayed on the screen at the front of my classroom, and that they should be working on it *before* the bell rings. Of course, to begin their warm-up, they'll have already dealt with having a pencil that is sharp.

Having our students working before the bell rings saves us a significant amount of time during the first five minutes of class, keeps students engaged, and eliminates the need to constantly remind them what they should be doing.

3. **Grab their attention.** What do you prefer: a waiter who mumbles a monotone "hello," then rambles off the specials, bored and looking at the ceiling — or one who enthusiastically explains each dish in juicy detail, engages us in conversation, and throws in a joke or compliment?

   Students, especially our at-risk students, need something more than just being talked at.

   Consider engaging their minds *and* bodies with an opening clap ("Welcome everyone, let's start out with a 2-clap on the count of three. Ready? 1, 2, 3…").

   Or perhaps tell a funny story that happened to you on the way home from school yesterday. You don't have to be Jay Leno with an opening monologue, but a quick joke, a short video clip, or an interesting news story that relates to what you are going to teach can all be excellent attention grabbers.

4. **Provide purpose.** Why do you choose to eat in any particular establishment — do you need filling, comfort food, a light, quick meal, or something spicy and exotic? You always have a reason or purpose for what you choose to eat. And, while students can't necessarily choose what they are going to learn on a given day, they can certainly

understand whether what they are learning has a purpose or not.

It's our job, as teachers, to help our students see the purpose at the beginning of each class: *your students need to know why they're there.* Here are three steps for clearly communicating a lesson's purpose to students:

*__Write it:__ Have your objective clearly posted in the same, accessible place each day. Make sure it is student-friendly language!

For example:

(not student-friendly)
Objective: The students will be able to calculate measures of central tendency.

(student-friendly)
Objective: We will calculate mean, median and mode, and be able to describe each to a friend.

*__Say it:__ In a straightforward manner, tell your students (most effective if done so while pointed to it in the written form indicated above): "By the end of class today, you will be able to calculate mean, median and mode. You'll know you can do this because you will be able to tell a friend how to do it, as well as do it by yourself using a pencil and paper."

Here is where you can also connect the lesson to a larger purpose in their lives: "Believe it or not, you will use these skills when you are doing real things in your life such as shopping for houses and negotiating salaries."

*__Ask for it back:__ Have the students tell you why they're here. After completing the above two, simply ask a student aloud: "Hey Brandon, please tell us why we're here today."

5. **Cut the hypocrisy.** Would you trust a server at a health food restaurant who looks run down and out of shape? Or one at a five-star restaurant who dresses sloppily and speaks incorrectly? This goes beyond appearances, and deeper to authenticity. In short: we can't truly sell what we don't truly embody.

Often, I see teachers chatting in the halls, texting, or running to/from the copy machine as the final bell rings. Admittedly, I've done all of these things as well. However, when we do, we severely weaken the power we have to insist that our students get to class on time, be ready to learn, and stay attuned to what we're asking them to do.

The key to our students being well-prepared, curious and passionate human beings begins with us, as teachers, being the same.

For me, this classic story perfectly illustrates our role as teachers (and gurus?):

A troubled mother took her daughter to see Mohandas Gandhi, who was world-renowned for his great spiritual discipline. It seems the young girl had become addicted to eating sweets, and her mother wanted Gandhi to speak to her about this harmful habit and convince her to drop it. Upon hearing this request, Gandhi paused in silence and then told the mother, "Bring the girl back to me in three weeks and I will speak to her then."

Just as she was instructed, the mother returned with her daughter, and Gandhi, as he had promised, spoke to the girl about the detrimental effects of eating too many sweets. He counseled her to give them up.

The mother gratefully thanked Gandhi, but was perplexed.

"Why," she asked him, "did you not speak to my daughter when we first came to you?"

"My good woman," Gandhi replied, "three weeks ago, I myself was still addicted to sweets!"

So, next time you step into your classroom, notice what you do in the first five minutes of your class to make an impression. Remember the restaurant analogy and serve your students some appetizing learning from the moment they walk in the door!

4

PLEASE STOP THINKING!

FOUR THINGS TEACHERS SAY
THAT SABOTAGE LEARNING

As teachers, we always keep an eye out for the "teachable moment." Those unexpected twists and turns (usually student-provoked) in our daily routine that allow us to grab hold of a question, comment or mistake and spark in our students knowledge that is real-time and interesting.

We're also taught to ask questions that are thought-provoking and lead to "higher-level" conversations. As a basic premise, we know that the teachable moment is often the most powerful, memorable part of our day.

However, often below that knowledge are words, phrases and instructions that do *the exact opposite* of what we intend. Instead of invoking thinking, these words actually sabotage it. Bringing these phrases to our consciousness can help us truly take advantage of teachable moments and inspire learning in our classrooms.

WHAT NOT TO SAY

Below are four of these phrases (as spoken by the teacher), how they are perceived (as heard by the students), and a few alternatives that will keep your classes on-track, on-target and ready for the next truly teachable moment.

1. **What we say:** "You were supposed to have learned this last year."

   What students hear: "You didn't do what you were supposed to do last year, and it doesn't appear that you're doing it this year either."

   In addition, when we make this statement, we are also implying that the teacher that they had last year didn't do their job properly. This creates a negative divide between you and the previous teacher, as well as you and the students. In addition, often the student(s) *did* learn it last year, they just don't recognize it because it is now in a different context with a different teacher.

   Instead consider the following alternatives:

   > "I believe you have *some* background knowledge about this concept. Tell me some of the things you know about xx."

   > "Let's step back from this topic and look at some of the information we need to know in order to understand this."

   > "Let me see a show of hands of who *does* remember this (half the class). OK, now those of you raising your hands have 3 minutes to pair up with those who do not, and tell them everything you know about this topic."

   All three of the above statements take the responsibility of learning away from whatever happened (or did *not* happen) last year, and instead refocus the learning on the students, what they already know, and what they need to know. In addition, it does so in a way that is empowering for the students.

2. **What we say:** "This is important. It will be on the test."

   What students hear: "Don't worry about all that other stuff. If I don't tell you it's on the test, it's not really something we need to focus on."

Tests, like grades, are important. But we all know that the best way to do well on tests and get good grades is to *learn, understand and apply* the information. In addition, any student with a history of poor grades is not motivated by what will be on the test. She is motivated by knowing how the information you're teaching in class will help her in her life. As teachers, one of our goals is to instill in our students a personal engagement in the subject we are teaching them.

This statement also undermines us as teachers. Placing the information's importance on the fact that it will be tested also sends the message that it is the only reason we're teaching it, that we are not in control of our curriculum, and we ourselves do not understand its importance.

Instead consider the following alternatives:

> "This is important. It helps us understand the link between x and y."

> "Tomorrow, we're going to study y. Let's make sure we understand x, so that we can easily understand the connection when we uncover it tomorrow."

> "I didn't think that this was important when I learned it in school. But then one day I (insert your own story here!)."

All three of the above take the emphasis off of the test, and promote the importance of a love of learning, as well as lifelong learning. They help our students make connections within the subject matter, as well as connections between the information and their daily lives. When true learning happens, the test scores and grades seem to take care of themselves!

3. **What we say:** "Please stop talking."
   What students hear: "Please stop talking… and thinking!"

Yes, there are times when we need the students to stop talking so that we can give instructions. And there are times when personal issues are of greater interest to our students than the teacher's objectives for the day.

But there are also times when the students *really are* talking about the subject matter. And when we demand that they stop talking, we are, many times, demanding that in order to be quiet, they switch from a brain filled with ideas and questions to one that is blank and uninterested.

Instead consider the following alternatives to quiet down or transition your class (and keep them thinking at the same time):

> "I am going to count down from 10. In those ten seconds I want you to read the objective on the board, and be prepared to discuss it." (promotes reading)

> "If you can hear me, clap once. If you can hear me, clap twice." (promotes kinesthetics)

> "As I lower my hand, change your conversations into a soft whisper, until my hand is lowered completely." (Note: This one requires a bit of training in advance, but I have found kids love the participation of it. I liken it to how the end of a song fades into silence, as opposed to being turned off abruptly.)

Students talk when they are excited. And in today's non-stop world of texting and social networking, the floodgates seem always open for them to comment, reply or "like" (Facebook users will understand that term) — a continuous kind of "talking" in the online world in which they're used to participating. The trick is to transition student

talking into learning the subject at hand, in a way
that is smooth, effective, engaging to the students and
respectful toward the teacher.

4. **What we say:** "Why didn't you do your homework?"
    What students hear: "Quick: think of something to say
    to get the teacher out of here as soon as possible!"

It's the age-old cliché, isn't it? *The dog ate it. My brother
ripped it. I did it, but I forgot to bring it.* We've heard
them all. And the reason we keep getting the same
old answers is because we keep asking the same old
question.

As famous sales guru Zig Ziglar says, "Failure is an event —
not a person." When a student does not do his homework,
focus on the act and the decision, not the individual or
personality type. Treat failure to complete homework as
a decision or as an event, and immediately move toward a
solution-based approach.

*Did the student write the homework down in class the previous
day? Is the student required to care for younger siblings, and
thus has little or no time to complete the work? Is the student
leaving her homework until late in the evening when she is
exhausted?*

I once had a student confess to me (after his fourth after-
school detention for not doing homework) that he had lost
his math book. As soon as we got him a new book, the
problem magically disappeared! Asking the right questions
can help uncover the truth, as well as some real solutions.

Instead consider the following alternatives:

> "If you could re-live yesterday, what would you do
> differently in order to get your homework done?"

"If you could change one thing about where and when you do your homework, what would that one thing be?"

"What are the biggest obstacles to you not getting your homework done?"

As teachers, we know that homework is the key to mastering concepts that we teach in class (often in a very limited amount of time). I often tell my students, "You haven't learned something until you can do it on your own, without my help."

Completing their homework is an essential part of this process. When we ask questions that focus on process and success, not failure, we can truly empower our students to achieve inside and outside of the classroom.

In sum, if we really want to seize those "teachable moments" with our students, we must be willing to put ourselves in their shoes and examine our own vernacular for those phrases that sabotage their learning. Then, we must erase those phrases from our teaching vocabulary and redirect them into words that inspire and empower our students to think beyond what they've been hearing for years, and engage in their own learning.

5

I said be Quiet... and start Talking!

HOW TO HELP STUDENTS LEARN OUT LOUD — AND STILL KEEP A HANDLE ON YOUR CLASSROOM

Recently, I had the opportunity to visit one of our state's lowest performing schools. Located in a high-poverty neighborhood, with a high percentage of minority students and test scores in the gutter, the school has all of the stereotypical low-performing attributes. *Except one.* There are relatively **no** behavior or discipline problems, according to school staff.

As I toured from classroom to classroom, I had to agree. The students seemed very well-behaved, and the teachers seemed to have their procedures and routines down to a science. As bells rang, the students moved through the halls with grace and ease. "I don't get it," one faculty member said to me, "We teach hard all day, but this is never reflected in our test scores."

As I continued to observe classrooms, I realized that the teachers absolutely were teaching. And that was the problem. The teachers spent so much time teaching, there was very little time left to devote to the students' *learning*.

By this, I mean, I did not see time devoted to discussion and interaction between teachers and students, or between students and their peers. The students' only learning option was to absorb lectures. How many of us learn best this way?

41

we can't fear student participation

With the rise of the Internet, social media and video recording capabilities on every machine we can fit into our pockets, today's students are social beings by necessity. They are constantly talking, texting and giving their opinions.

However, in schools, they are often asked to put this aside and be quiet — in order to "let the teacher teach." We often force students into roles in which they are expected to be quiet for an hour or more at a time, and then we expect them to remember everything we just said.

As teachers, we're often afraid that letting the students talk means risking giving up control of the classroom, and we fear that it will become difficult to reclaim that control in the middle of class. In their book, *Checking for Understanding*, authors Fisher and Frey report that in classrooms with more low-performing or English-language-learning students, there is an even higher rate of "teachers talking more and students talking less."

Giving into this fear of the "messiness" that may ensue when we engage students in interactive conversations is a disservice to them. Forgetting that English language learners likely have more advanced creative thinking abilities than may come through in their English speaking or writing is, too.

To ensure that our students learn the information we present to them, we need to give them time to *interact with* the information, including discussing, questioning and even arguing and flubbing it.

It's OK if it gets messy, and it does not have to mean chaos.

win-win strategies to get students talking

The following three strategies can help get students engaging with and discussing the curriculum they're learning — while allowing teachers to keep control of the classroom.

1. **Think-pair-share.** Developed by University of Maryland professor Frank Lyman, this strategy encourages students to do exactly what the name suggests. Here's how it works:

> *Think.* Begin by prompting the students to think about a concept or idea, or provide a specific question. Then give the students a minute to think in silence. The students can also jot down notes about their thoughts as well.
>
> One minute of "think" time is usually plenty; anything over a minute risks losing the momentum toward the desired outcome. Giving this wait time also eliminates eager students shouting out their answers, which often become the only answer that the rest of the students then give. It also decreases the chances of a student "hiding" at their desk in hopes that they will not be called upon.
>
> *Pair.* Next, prompts the students to turn to a partner(s) to discuss their individual thoughts (or written notes). It is very important that you be visible during this time, either by circulating the room, or sitting in on conversations you predict may be unfocused.
>
> You can also add urgency to the conversations by putting a time limit on them (i.e., "You have one minute to discuss your thoughts with your partner..."). In addition, it's helpful to have the students know who their partner is in advance of beginning this process. This helps the students stay focused on the conversation at hand, and eliminates the potential for one student to sit alone quietly while the rest of the class engages in conversation.
>
> As students share their answers, they do so in a situation that is much safer than saying it aloud for the first time

in front of the entire class. Should they find that their answer is completely off base, they can quickly make the adjustment, and have a better answer by the time the entire class discusses it.

However, more often than not, the students find that their answer is in line with what their partner was thinking, giving them confidence to move into the "share" phase.

Share. Next, call for pairs to share their discussion with the entire class. There are several options for having students share aloud, including:

- Simply calling on those who offer to share.

- Calling on all groups in a "round robin" format.

- Calling on individual students. A deeper step is to ask an individual student to share only what their partner talked about. This insures not only that the students were talking to one another, but that they were listening to each other as well.

Note: Add to the depth of the learning by recording key points on the overhead or white board. This also provides a running record that the students can access later to reinforce their learning.

2. **Three questions** More popularly referred to by my students as "Interrogator," this strategy is designed to get students to break from the traditional "pre-canned questions" format that is often used in interviewing. It helps them truly listen to their partner's response before moving on to the next question.

In addition, this strategy also compels students who are answering the questions to speak in a way that gives their partner enough depth and content to construct a new question.

Here's how it works:

Part I: Student A asks her partner, Student B, three questions.

The first question is provided by you, the teacher (as students develop this skill, they can create their own first question). The second question is then asked by Student A, but must build upon the answer received from the first question. Student A then asks a third question, based on her partner's answer to her second question.

Student A may ONLY ask questions. Student B must provide ONLY answers, and must speak in full sentences.

Part II: Student B asks the questions, starting with the first one (teacher provided).

The rigor of conversation can be increased by not allowing Student B to ask the same questions that *they* were asked for the second and third question.

Here's an example of how this conversation might look in an 11th grade English class that is discussing *Walden*:

> *Student A* (teacher-prompted): What does it mean when Thoreau says, "I would rather sit on a pumpkin and have it all to myself, than be crowded on a velvet cushion."
>
> *Student B:* I think it means that that it is better to have something that is cheap all to yourself, than to share something expensive with a lot of other people.
>
> *Student A:* Have you ever had something that was cheap all to yourself?

45

Student B: When I was younger, my brother got a new bike, and I got his old one. Nobody asked me to try the old bike, but everyone wanted to try my brother's new bike.

Student A: If you had the choice, would you rather have had the old bike, or the new bike?

Student B: Actually, my brother left the new bike at the park, and somebody took it. So I guess Thoreau is right!

3. **Record it!** By demanding that our students put their Smart Phones away (while rolling our eyes), we are actually neglecting an extremely valuable tool to help our students speak, especially our English language learners. We're also missing an opportunity to "meet students where they live" and help them engage with technology in an educational way.

With most electronic gadgets containing the ability to record voice these days, having students read or speak into their recording device helps them to practice communicating in a way that is private and non-threatening.

Here are three activities students can do:

- With many classrooms now having a set of i-Pods available to them, students can easily record themselves reading a passage, and listen to it at their convenience, as many times as necessary. They can then make adjustments to their reading, re-record themselves, and hear the difference. Also consider pairing up a weak speaker with a strong one, in order for the weaker speaker to hear the same passage read by a strong voice.

- When the teacher asks a question, students record themselves speaking the answer. When called upon, a reluctant speaker can simple hit "play" for their partner, or for the class to hear their pre-recorded response.

- Consider extending this activity by using a computer application, such as "Sonic Pics" (available at http://www.sonicpics.com/) to have students record their voice over photographs and create a narrated slide show. These apps are extremely easy to use, highly engaging for the students, and very effective. An added benefit is that since students are recording their every word, they are much more likely to stick to the academic content that the teacher insists on!

LeT THem LeaRn OUT LOUD

While reading and writing are incredibly important to the success of our students, for many, the ability to speak well will help them not only achieve in school, but throughout their lives. According to Harvey MacKay, author of the book, *Swim with the Sharks*, "The number one skill most lacking in business today is public speaking — the ability to present oneself."

Our students' ability to learn hinges on their ability to speak their minds and process their thoughts aloud. The ability to speak well allows them to present themselves in a confident manner in the world, and gives them the potential to truly achieve the promise that we hold for them.

As teachers, we must have the courage to stop "teaching at" our students for hours on end, and make the space for them to learn out loud, from their own voices and from one another.

6

IT'S TEST TIIIIIMe!!!

STRATEGIES FOR THINKING "OUTSIDE THE BUBBLE" ON THE ALL-IMPORTANT STANDARDIZED TESTS

It's that time again. Time to start training your students to fill in the bubbles that matter most (whether they are literal bubbles on paper or the new computerized versions!).

Like it or not, for most teachers, those literal or figurative bubbles determine in large part the public's perceptions of our school and district, our students' opinions of themselves, and our school site's administrators (who may change, for better or worse, once test results come in). In some places, those test scores also determine whether or not we are considered "highly effective" teachers, regardless of where and whom we teach.

Perhaps you see standardized test scores as either not at all or truly indicative of your students' capabilities, and yours. Or perhaps you see them as another reason why "high-performing" schools will continue to flourish, while other schools continue to languish.

Or, like most great teachers I know, perhaps you see these tests as a necessary nuisance — and while you know they don't tell the whole story, you do see the value in having the students try their best, and attain the highest scores they can. If nothing else, you realize that, given the current state of affairs, *not* preparing your students to achieve on these tests could negatively impact their future, your school's future, and even your own.

So, I offer you four "out-of-the-bubble" strategies to help you focus on this practical picture of standardized test time, and to go further than just having your students "use the answers to work backwards" to prepare for the all-important tests ahead.

1. **Remember: It's not about perfection — it's about improvement.** I usually begin my standardized test prep about a month before the tests begin, and I start by showing my students their results from last year.

    For my particular at-risk students, this usually means a short black line, compared to the much longer line showing how "the rest of the state" performed. Instead of having them focus on *their* line, I have them use a highlighter to highlight the area that is open for them to *improve*.

    Our state's students are ranked as either "far below basic," "below basic," "basic," "proficient" or "advanced." While my students usually fall into one of the first two categories, what often goes unrealized is this: whatever category your students are in, to move up one or two levels, they usually *only need to answer a few more questions correctly.* Some only missed the next level by a question or two.

    I then prompt them with the following questions:

    1. *Think about how much smarter you are right now than you were last year at this time. Can you answer (insert number) more questions correctly than you did last year?* Most students will nod confidently, and some will be quite motivated by how easily they could move up a level or two.

    2. *What can you begin doing to make this happen?* Guide them by making a list that includes everything from getting some more sleep to looking over tests they have taken throughout the year and reviewing what they previously missed.

When your students (and you) realize that you can focus on just a *small step of improvement* — whether it's moving into "basic" or "advanced" — the tests become less daunting and you can focus on what needs to be done.

2. **Focus on celebration, not intimidation.** I have seen first-hand the positive results when we take a positive, even celebratory, approach to testing with students.

    As "The Rappin' Mathematician," several years ago I created a song called "Test Tiiiiiime!" to help get our school motivated to take the test. Using the song — which playfully asks: "What time is it?" and answers "It's test tiiiiiime!" — our school's video club actually made a rap video with students as the stars, and we played it on our closed-circuit television each morning.

    The whole school was so pumped up for testing it was amazing, and our test results reflected it. A teacher from another school told me that while they didn't make a video, their principal played the song over the loudspeaker each morning, and even some of the administrators were caught breakdancing in the halls! (You can download this song from my website, www.alexkajitani.com.)

    What exactly is there to celebrate about testing, you ask? As an 8th grade math teacher, one of my biggest challenges is that by the time test scores are released, my students have already moved on to another school, and a completely different set of students now sit in front of me. This will hopefully change as tests become computerized, and results are generated much more quickly.

    But, in any case, it's important to celebrate parts of test-taking that aren't just the results, so students feel empowered to try their best, and proud of their focus and effort. For example, we can reward the following:

1. Perfect attendance during testing days.
2. Being well-rested and eating a healthy breakfast.
3. Not finishing too quickly, and checking over all of their answers.
4. Not leaving any answers blank.

3. **Involve the whole school community.** There are no limits to who should be involved in the testing process. Make sure everyone on your campus knows about, and celebrates, the testing period.

As students purchase their lunch, have the cafeteria staff wish them good luck. Have the maintenance staff talking to students about it, and non-core teachers should be celebrating their importance as well. Our middle school always thanks our elementary feeder schools for their hard work, and the local high school always thanks us.

Of course, parents must be included and encouraged to support their students' test-taking, via meetings or notes or phone calls home. Even local businesses can be informed about testing, so that when school-aged kids come into their establishments, they can also encourage them. When students see that their whole communities want them to succeed, they are more motivated and accountable to try their best, which is all we can ask of them.

4. **Think the tests are racially biased or favor the affluent? Then get real and talk to your students about it.** If you teach at-risk students, this tip is especially relevant to you. Most states' department of education websites make test results available by school, district, income level and race.

They often include research comparisons and commentary on how African-American, Latino and Native American students perform, compared to their White and Asian-American counterparts, as well as results from poor neighborhoods compared to affluent ones. Use these numbers as both eye-openers and motivators for your at-risk students.

If possible, find a school in a poor neighborhood that has stellar test scores (or something equally inspiring to your demographic). Then, once you've compiled this information, *share it with your students.* Don't be intimidated to open up the discussion about why you, or your students, believe certain ethnicities score lower or higher on the tests.

Keep the conversation respectful but real. Encourage them to rise above the low test scores that have plagued their school, their neighborhood, or their ethnicity.

If possible, and if time allows, take this conversation a step further by showing statistics on unemployment by race, as well as high school graduation and college entrance rates, and lifetime earnings. Discuss how and why academic performance is measured, and tie it in with success throughout life.

Give your students the opportunity to see the big picture beyond these test bubbles, as you do, and give them credit in their ability to be motivated by their futures.

In closing, we may never love the emphasis on standardized test scores in our current system, but we can at least make the best of things — by taking a positive and strategic approach to preparing them for test success. Here's wishing you, your students, your school, district and community a happy and fruitful testing season.

"What time is it? It's Test Tiiiiime!!!"

7

Dealing With Data

How to Transform Your Perception of Data and Help Your Students Succeed

What single factor ultimately determines whether a student is an at-risk student?

It's not work ethic, as we all know students who don't like to work hard, but are still bright enough to make it through high school and even college. It's not ethnicity, as we all know students of different ethnicities who are low, and high, achievers. Nor is it gender, socioeconomics or the neighborhood they live in.

What ultimately determines whether a student is an at-risk student is *the data we have collected on them.*

Low test scores, year after year, have labeled more students "at-risk" than any other single factor. In California, like in many states, students are labeled as "Far Below Basic, Below Basic, Basic, Proficient, or Advanced." A student who consistently scores in the "Far Below Basic" category is indicative of a student at risk for dropping out of school.

Of course, embedded in labels such as these are a multitude of complex factors such as work ethic, home life, socioeconomics and ethnicity. But, at the end of the day, it is the *test data* that determines the label in official terms.

This school year, as part of my duties as a Teacher on Special Assignment for my school district, I am charged with the task of helping our district actually use our masses of collected data to help students, teachers, administrators and schools improve and succeed. This task has been nothing short of enlightening — and inspiring — for me, and my perceptions of data have certainly shifted.

I now view data as having incredibly positive potential for our schools (as opposed to the darker side of data that puts us teachers on the constant defensive). As I go into our schools each week and talk with fellow educators about how we can actually use all this data we collect — in big and small ways, in our classrooms and offices each day — I'm seeing many of their perceptions begin to shift as well.

HOW DO WE DEFINE DATA?

Businesses have always relied on sales data to reward and fire employees, project future earnings and plan strategically. Politicians have always relied on data, and many an election has been won (and lost!) based on effective use of data.

As an industry, education is just beginning to grasp the importance of analyzing data to help our schools and students achieve. However, most of the data analysis methods that we use have been learned "on the job," as traditional credential programs have not required data analysis coursework as part of their requirements.

Data, as defined by the *Merriam-Webster Dictionary*, is "Factual information used as a basis for reasoning, discussion or calculation." In other words, it is not limited to just numbers, and data on our students does not just come to us in the form of spreadsheets and statistics.

Data is information, and information that can be used to help our students is the best kind. Thus, although test scores are the most talked-about form of data in education, we needn't limit "data collection" to that. Think of data as any factual information that can help us reach students.

HOW can we actually use Data?

Here, I offer four strategies that educators can use to effectively use data to better understand your students, respond to their needs, and redirect them onto the path to success as quickly as possible:

In Your Classroom

1. **Data should be used to *begin* a conversation, not to end it.** As educators, we have an obligation to believe that all students can learn. Too often, we use data to justify why a student *can't learn*, as opposed to using it as a lens through which we can carefully plan instruction.

   Consider the following examples of using data as the beginning, versus the end, of a conversation:

as THE enD OF a conversation...	as THE BeGInnInG OF a conversation...
"Gerald is a 'far below basic' student; he is going to have trouble completing this activity."	"Gerald scored 'far below basic' on our last test; what strategies can I use to help him complete this activity?"
"Half of my class is currently reading below grade level. I doubt we'll be able to hit all of the state standards this year."	"With half of my class reading below grade level, I need to find ways to help them close the achievement gap, while at the same time challenging my students who are reading at grade level."
"Two-thirds of my students' parents never finished high school. They won't be able to help their students with their homework."	"Two-thirds of my students' parents never finished high school. What additional resources are available to help them?"

While the above examples may seem obvious in their nature, it is often too easy for us teachers-under-pressure to make excuses for why our students aren't achieving, and use the data to back up our thoughts.

Instead of using data to make statements, *use data to ask questions.*

2. **Remember, behind every piece of data is a real student.** Last year, when analyzing some test scores, I noticed that one of my student's scores had dropped significantly from his previous two test scores. I also noticed that he had not turned in some of his homework for the unit (he usually did). When I presented him with the data, he confided that his parents were splitting up, and that he hadn't been sleeping much over the past two weeks.

    While I was not well-informed on this student's life at home, because I was familiar with his data, I was able to quickly identify what he needed, and arranged for him to meet with the counselor. And while the following months were a challenge to keep him focused on his academics, something that would have normally put him at-risk for failing instead put him "at-promise," and he passed all his courses.

    When we accept the data as real, then we accept it as a part of our students' lives. Every piece of data tells a story. As teachers, it is our job to identify and understand those stories.

3. **Data kept secret is useless (and even damaging).** With so many school districts moving toward a "value added" method of evaluating teachers, it is no surprise that many teachers are hesitant to share their data. It can be frightening in today's climate. However, as educators, we must get past the stigma that "bad data" automatically means "bad teacher."

Here's what I've learned: using data to truly help students succeed requires a *group effort* of teachers and administrators.

When teachers work in a collaborative climate that encourages open communication around data, a teacher whose students scored low on a particular section of a recent test can identify teachers whose students scored well on that portion, and seek out their guidance and wisdom. A teacher whose students scored particularly well on a given portion should always be tapped to share their pedagogical practices, to elevate the teaching practices of the entire department.

Let's use data to identify areas of strengths and weakness in our individual students, as well as with our students overall, and choose as a profession to shift our perception of data as our enemy to that of *another colleague working with us to help our students succeed.* Each time we do this, our students will ultimately benefit the most.

4. **When possible, use analogies.** A colleague of mine recently described the achievement gap in a way that made everyone in the room understand it clearly. He said:

    > "Imagine all of the students except ours get in a big bus, and the bus takes off down the highway going 60 miles per hour. An hour later, our students get in a bus, which takes off going down the same highway, but at 50 miles per hour. Not only is that bus an hour behind, but at the rate it is going, our students will never catch up.

    > The distance between the two buses is the achievement gap, and the only way to catch up to the first bus is to accelerate the bus, thus accelerating the learning."

As everyone in the room nodded their heads in agreement, my colleague had brilliantly used a simple analogy to explain something as complex as the achievement gap, to which so many of our at-risk students fall prey.

Learning from this method, I recently used the following analogy to explain formative versus summative assessments:

"What's the difference between an autopsy and an MRI?" (Long pause to give everyone in the room some think time.) "An autopsy is used after someone has died. It is used to answer the question, 'What happened?' While the results can be informative, there is no way to save the patient. All we can do is use the information we gain from the autopsy to hopefully help others in the future.

This is similar to our end-of-year (summative) State Assessments. We get the results, but by then, it's too late. The students have moved on to another grade, and we're quite limited in what we can do with the information.

On the other hand, an MRI is used to identify areas of weakness, and allows us to act in a timely manner, prescribing a course of action for treatment to help a patient survive. In education terms, treatment means prescribing intervention strategies that will get our at-risk students on the right path before they drop out. This is effectively using formative assessment."

Like digging up the stories behind the data, I have found that creating analogies to describe the often-complex kinds and uses of data helps make it less intimidating, and helps us all understand how we can truly use data in positive ways to help our students.

Make Friends With Data

In sum, data is information that is valuable, useful and crucial to the success of our students, and to our own success as educators. By incorporating the above four techniques into your daily practice, you may find that your perception of the positive potential of data begins to shift dramatically. I truly hope it does, because as educators today, our choice is to either let data be our downfall, or to embrace data and use it to elevate our profession and our students.

PART ONE

TEACHER AS CLASSROOM LEADER

Part One, Section 2:
Special Strategies for Succeeding
With At-Risk and Struggling
Students and Populations

8

IT'S ABOUT TIME

CLOSING THE ACHIEVEMENT GAP
WITH AT-RISK STUDENTS

A few years ago, I had an 8th grade student named Eduardo. Eduardo was constantly being poked fun at by his classmates for his inability to do simple things, such as add and subtract, or tie his shoes. His grades were very low in all of his classes, and for as long as he or his mother could remember, he had always failed in all subjects.

One day in class, I heard a student tell Eduardo, "You are so dumb, you don't even know how to tell time!" As he shriveled in his seat, I walked over to Eduardo and quietly asked him if that was true. I then asked him the most simple, yet profound question a teacher can ask: *Why?*

Not allowing him to shrug his shoulders and say, "I don't know," I pressed him for an answer. Finally, he exclaimed, "Nobody ever taught me!" "What about your parents?" I asked. "Nope." he replied.

I then proceeded to take the clock off the wall, and explain how it worked. Within 10 minutes, Eduardo knew how to tell time. For 10 years, nobody had ever taken 10 minutes to show him how it worked.

Many had simply dismissed Eduardo as "unable to learn." He could learn. In fact, he learned quickly and well, and I told him so.

After that day, his confidence began to increase. He became interested in learning, because he knew he could. He began doing his homework, and even started performing better on tests.

ReaL CHILDReN IN THe meTaPHORICaL GaP

The "Achievement Gap" has become a popular buzzword for students performing below, often far below, their expected grade-level proficiency. However, for these students, the achievement gap is not a buzzword — it is a devastating disadvantage that, if left unaddressed, can severely undermine a student's opportunity to live a successful life.

For many at-risk students like Eduardo, the achievement gap begins well before kindergarten. It begins at home with parents who are not literate, or who do not speak English. It begins in neighborhoods where the concern over whether the family will eat that night far outweighs reading a book to the children before bed.

And as a child's education begins, the gap often continues to grow. As teachers, we spend significant amounts of time trying to "catch them up," instead of focusing solely on the grade level standards. A student who achieves only half a year's growth for each year they are in school may be six or more grade levels below where they should be by the time they need to pass the High School Exit Exam.

Yet the deep effects of the achievement gap extend far beyond a student passing this test. As a society, we cannot afford to produce 18-year olds who have only a 6th grade education. We cannot allow an achievement gap that preys upon our ethnic minorities, especially our Latino and African-American students, to persist. Not addressing this gap means not addressing many of the economic and racial disparities that exist, for real children, in our society.

Fortunately, there are resolutions. While these resolutions are deep, varied, and highly debated, the ones we can most affect begin with us, the teachers.

FOUR STRATEGIES TO HELP CLOSE THE GAP IN YOUR CLASSROOM

Here are four strategies you can use *now* in your own classroom, and at your school, to work toward closing the achievement gap for at-risk students:

1. **Teach curriculum that is culturally relevant.** Let's be honest: a 14-year old minority student living below the poverty line relates much differently to the world than a white student living in an affluent neighborhood. With life experiences so different, why would we even attempt to teach them the same way?

    Recently, when discussing percentages, our class pushed aside the standard curriculum to instead discuss dropout, graduation, and unemployment rates among Latino students, as well as differences in percentages of minority students attending college. By making percentages culturally relevant, the students were able to see that percentages are a math concept that most definitely applies directly to their lives, and their futures.

2. **Keep good teachers at your school.** Getting high-quality teachers to come teach in schools with large achievement gaps is tough. Getting them to stay is even tougher.

    Nationally, the average turnover for all teachers is 17 percent, and in urban schools, 20 percent. That means that in schools like mine (and many of yours), we are replacing 1 out of every 5 teachers *every single year.*

    You can be part of the solution to this turnover problem (which, by the way, the National Education Association estimates is costing our schools $7 billion a year). Be a team player. Offer to help or support fellow teachers; show your appreciation for what they do. Model commitment to and enthusiasm for teaching at-risk students, and remind your colleagues publicly what a difference they make and important job they have.

It may sound trite, but it is critical that we keep all teachers motivated and included to solve this educational crisis.

3. **Get targeted training.** Advocate for professional development at your school site that addresses sociological as well as practical issues. Become an expert not only on how to overcome teaching challenges, but on the larger issues surrounding your students as well — poverty, racism, and gang recruitment.

    One of the best staff development meetings we ever had was when the gang-prevention officer from our local police department came and spoke to our staff about his job and its challenges. I learned more from his presentation about the neighborhood in which I teach than I had in all the years I'd been teaching there. Call your local police department, and ask about scheduling something similar.

4. **Connect with the quiet ones.** The students slipping through the cracks aren't usually the ones all the teachers know; they are the ones whose faces are fuzzy in our brains because their presence in the classroom is barely felt.

    I saw one of my middle school students from last year, who fit that description, crossing the street in front of my car recently. She was noticeably pregnant. I couldn't remember her name, and I realized that I had failed her.

    Of course, it is a conglomeration of many circumstances that make these students fall from our grasp, but don't be a contributing factor. Go into your classroom tomorrow, notice each "quiet one" and find a way to connect.

Closing the achievement gap takes time, commitment, and understanding of the larger cultural and educational issues, as well as the "smaller" issues that may be happening in an individual student's life, neighborhood and home. It takes stopping and asking: *Why?* And then working, 10 minutes at a time, one student at a time, to address a deficit that may have begun long before that student even started school.

In all honesty, I'm not sure what happened with Eduardo. As his life moved on beyond middle school, we did not keep in contact. But at least I know that the next person who asks him for the time will not be disappointed in his answer. And that's a start.

9

LeT'S TaLK aBOUT Race

HOW TO BRING eTHNIC IDENTITY, aND CULTURaLLY-ReLeVaNT CURRICULUM, INTO OUR CLaSSROOMS

In Your Classroom

Scene One: *It's 7:30 a.m. on a chilly Tuesday morning, and I'm unlocking the door to my classroom. David (pronounced dah-veed), one of my top students, runs up to me and begins profusely apologizing. "Mr. Kajitani, I'm so sorry, I didn't do my homework last night." Not one to miss his homework assignments, I question him as to why. "My uncle was at work last night, and 'la migra' (what my Mexican-American students call the Immigration and Naturalization Service) came to his work and hauled him away. They put him on a bus back to Mexico, and my aunt, who lives with us, was freaking out all night. I couldn't get to my homework."*

Scene Two *At 3 p.m. that same day, at the math department meeting, one of our teachers is distraught because she has just been accused of being a "racist" by one of her students. She explains: "I was describing one of our students, and I said, 'he's a short, black kid with glasses.' Another student immediately shouted, 'You're a racist!' I don't think using the term 'black' makes me a racist, but I didn't know what to say."*

If you teach in a school like mine, where minority students are the majority, yet most of the teachers are white, then it is highly likely that race and ethnicity play a large role in your school culture — even if (*especially* if) these topics are seldom talked about.

In a country still coming to grips with its first African-American president — and one who is not afraid to talk about race and ethnicity — we as teachers have the opportunity to create a world in which these critical topics are not something pushed aside, but rather a central part of our daily teachings.

We know now that "ignoring" race or being "colorblind" not only doesn't work, but actually *harms* — as it refuses to honor a major piece of the identity of every one of us (whether our ancestors come from Latin America, Africa, Europe, Asia or elsewhere). In fact, "colorblindness" is a position of privilege that has been called "the new racism," as it ignores the real experiences of others not in the majority culture.

The time has come to move past our discomfort, and "talk about race" in our classrooms and schools. More specifically, it's time to provide our students, especially our at-risk students, with a culturally relevant curriculum — one that incorporates our students' specific cultural backgrounds into our lessons, to help them thrive academically and personally.

WHERE TO BEGIN?

I get it: race and ethnicity are taboo, and thus uncomfortable, topics to discuss in our culture.

But, the good news is, there's a whole field of study within and outside of education, about how to understand and address these topics productively. This is the field I drew upon back in the day for my Master's thesis, which was about ethnic identity development — and it's the field of study and practice I still draw on today when coaching teachers to "talk about race."

There's even better news, too. As teachers, we have the ear of the next generations in our classroom each day. And if we can teach them to productively talk about race and ethnicity — and provide them with learning via culturally-relevant curriculum — then these topics won't be so volatile and uncomfortable in the future, as today's students become our cultural leaders.

So, here are three simple steps to start with, which can lay the foundation for you to open dialogue and introduce culturally-relevant curriculum in your classroom:

1. **Understand what ethnicity is.** While a multitude of academic definitions and debates exist surrounding the term, ethnicity is, at core, *your affiliation with* your race, country of origin, culture, language, family traditions and socioeconomics. A culturally relevant curriculum is one that takes the ethnicity of our students into consideration when designing lesson plans.

2. **Understand how ethnicity is formed.** Dr. Beverly Cross, a professor of urban education at the University of Memphis, created a five-stage model for understanding how our students of color go about forming their racial identity. For an enlightening and more in-depth look at Dr. Cross' model, I highly recommend reading Dr. Beverly Tatum's book, *Why Are All the Black Kids Sitting Together in the Cafeteria?*

   However, in an effort to understand our students better, here are the five stages in simple terms:

   1) **Pre-Encounter:** A person who is in the first stage, Pre-Encounter, hasn't really thought much about their own ethnicity, or the ethnicity of others. In fact, they're pretty happy to go along with what everyone else around them believes.

   2) **Encounter:** The encounter stage is usually not one that a person chooses to enter on their own, and is often triggered by an event or series of events, in which they are personally impacted by witnessing an act of racism, or by being the target of racism. Once in the Encounter Stage, a person can no longer fail to acknowledge that different races and ethnicities exist in the world.

3) **Immersion/Emersion:** In the immersion stage, a person begins to explore her ethnicity, and will often surround herself with *people and symbols of her same ethnicity*, such as jewelry, clothing, music and events, all of which convey messages about who they identify with. The person also begins to seek out opportunities to learn about his own history and culture, and might even begin to develop a great amount of pride in his race and ethnicity. For many people, this stage begins when they go to college.

4) **Internalization:** Once in the internalization stage, a person begins to gain a sense of security about her racial identity. With this security comes a willingness and openness to connect and establish relationships across racial lines.

5) **Internalization/Commitment:** In the fifth stage, a person makes a commitment to work toward furthering his own understanding of his race and ethnicity, as well as helping others to find their own understanding or meaning.

Of course, it should also be noted that the above five stages are not necessarily always linear, nor does everyone go through all of the stages. However, understanding the process that our students go through helps tremendously in our understanding of how we can use ethnicity to provide a culturally relevant curriculum.

3. **Understand how ethnicity can be used in the classroom.** So, what does all of the above information actually look like in our classrooms? The term "culturally-relevant curriculum" may sound complicated, but it really is simply bringing our students' cultures into our lessons in creative ways, which we all can do.

Here are some strategies and examples on where to begin:

1. ***Tell, ask, and connect.*** Tell your story, then ask the students for their story, then connect what they say to the subject or topic that you're covering in class.

   Our students, especially our students of color, actually love to talk about their ethnicity once you give them the chance. Often, it is we as teachers who are hesitant to talk about it (see "Scene Two" at the beginning of this article). Begin by simply telling the students about your ethnicity.

   Start bringing it up by addressing any of the following:

   • Who are you named after?
   • Where did your parents or grandparents come from?
   • What is your favorite family tradition?
   • What is *your* ethnicity?

   Also, be ready to "own" your own ethnicity when students ask. My last name is Japanese, and some people find it hard to pronounce. When any of my students, who are mostly Latino, ask me if they can call me "Mr. K" instead of "Mr. Kajitani," I tell them no. And then I tell them why — because I'm proud of my ethnicity, which is visible in my name. And I start a discussion about my students' names and how they can show pride in their ethnicity, too.

2. ***Turn numbers in people, who have ethnic identities.*** Once, as part of a unit on percentages, I asked my students to identify their race, and we calculated what percent of our class was white, black, Latino, etc. I then pulled up our school's website, and we compared those percentages with our overall school's percentages.

We then followed that up with percentage comparisons to our county of San Diego, state of California, and then the entire country. No longer were percentages a set of unconnected numbers and math symbols; rather, the students saw *themselves* in those numbers, instantly making them real and relevant to their lives.

3. *View arts and literature through a cultural and racial lens.*

Alan Sitomer, while teaching English in an inner-city high school in Los Angeles with large numbers of African-American students, brings similes to life by having students compare works by classic poets Langston Hughes and William Wordsworth to modern-day rappers such as Tupak Shakur and LL Cool J.

For example:

"What happens to a dream deferred?
Does it dry up
Like a raisin in the sun?"
(Langston Hughes)

Connects to:

"I'm stuck to my mattress like crazy glue"
(Tupak Shakur)

According to Sitomer, who wrote the book *Hip-Hop Poetry and the Classics,* as well as a series of novels geared toward students of color: "By taking popular artists seriously, we can build bridges of access and engagement to core academic concepts. This makes the content relevant and real to our students, and expands their world view in the process."

Clearly, these examples just scratch the surface of the myriad ways we can engage in "talking about race" and introducing culturally-relevant curriculum in our classrooms. But I hope they spark something for you, and provide you with some motivation and ideas to open this dialogue and integrate your students' ethnicity into your classroom lessons.

Once you're motivated, you can find exceptional teaching resources on this topic online, such as the free digital magazine, *Teaching Tolerance*, to which you can subscribe at www. tolerance. org; the NEA's "Diversity Toolkit"; and the PBS series *Race: The Power of Illusion*. There are also dozens of great books on the topic, such as Beverly Tatum's I mentioned above, Lisa Delpit's books, and many others.

Still, when I present this subject to teachers around the country, I feel people shifting in their seats with unease. But then, when I finish, without fail at least one audience member comes up to me and says emphatically, "*Thank you* for bringing up the topic of ethnicity!" and "That is *exactly* the process I went through myself, but I've never seen it put into words like that!"

I think, on a very deep level, we all benefit greatly from talking about race, and incorporating it into our classrooms. With a future in our country and our world that will be more and more ethnically diverse and interconnected, we do a great disservice by ignoring this topic in our classrooms. We have a responsibility to prepare our students as ethnically-aware and self-confident, multi-cultural citizens.

So, come on now, *"let's talk about race, bay-bee…"*

10

THE SECRET TO MOTIVATING THE UNMOTIVATED STUDENT

ONE KEY STRATEGY FOR SUCCEEDING WITH AT-RISK YOUTH

Let's be honest: As teachers, we often dread a lack of motivation in our students more than any other trait. And our at-risk students can be the most challenging cases, entering our classrooms with a multitude of family and sociological barriers, and often with well-established track records of low academic achievement.

Motivating a discouraged or disinterested student to achieve academically is a challenge that can be incredibly daunting.

But it can be done.

How do I know it can be done? Because *it is being done* by teachers, coaches and educators across the country.

How is it done? While of course this is a complicated issue, I've come to believe that there is *one main factor* behind any adult who successfully motivates the "unmotivated," at-risk, struggling students.

This main factor is simply this: *make real connections with them.* Build relationships. Help them feel seen. Believe in them. Have a stake in their success, and show it.

We can talk all we want about "not having time" or how many students we have — and all of this is true. But, if you knew that taking a few minutes each week to connect with a struggling, lost student could change the course of his or her life, would you do it? I bet you would.

a super success story

I had the pleasure of talking recently with Darrell "Coach D" Andrews. Coach D knows firsthand the plight of the at-risk student. Raised by a single mother on the public welfare system in Syracuse, New York, Coach D became a first-generation college graduate (an amazing feat considering the fact that he showed up on his college campus unregistered, with everything he owned in five garbage bags!).

Now, Coach D is a successful author, motivational coach and Certified Speaking Professional. When I asked him what critical factors led him down the path to college, rather than dropping out of high school, as most of the people he knew had done, here's what he told me:

> "Instead of looking at factors, I would like to look at people. One of my core philosophies regarding youth and students is simple: 'A student with a dream is a student with a future; however, a student with a dream is fueled by a caring adult who believes in their dream.'
>
> The two people who set the tone for my future were my mother, Constance, and my 6th grade teacher, Mrs. Palma."

Coach D went on to tell me how his mother chose to be an example to him when he was school-age, returning to school herself and becoming the first in the family to receive a high school diploma — showing her son it was worth doing. And Coach D's teacher, Mrs. Palma, "saw beyond the angry boy" he was, and told him she would never give up on him. He explained to me:

> "I was an at-risk youth who had a dream for a better life, and this dream was supported by caring adults.

I have been preaching from the mountaintops for years that we are putting the cart before the horse. Relationships build successful students. If you put anything else first, you will simply keep going in circles.

I am where I am today because of caring relationships, which then led to textbook excellence."

I can't think of a better example to show the power of this approach. So, what are some *concrete strategies* to build relationships with our at-risk students? Here are three:

THREE STRATEGIES TO CONNECT WITH OUR AT-RISK STUDENTS

1. **Understand and honor cultural barriers.** For years, while speaking sternly or reprimanding my mostly Latino students, I would get increasingly frustrated as I spoke to them and they would look away, seemingly uninterested in what I was saying. I would demand over and over that they, "Look at me while I'm talking to you."

   One day, a colleague witnessed me doing this, and explained that in most of the Latino cultures that our students come from, giving eye contact to a superior (i.e., the teacher) is actually considered very disrespectful. *Ooops.* It turns out our students aren't the only ones learning lessons each day!

   From that point on, I began teaching eye contact as a specific skill our students needed to learn, embedding it in weekly lessons.

   Just as we can't assume our students walk into our classrooms each day aware of every social norm, we also can't assume that the customs that we have been raised on are the same as those of our students. Get to know the cultural customs and nuances of the students you teach —

when you *ask* students about their culture you also make deeper connections with them. And remember, the key is to *incorporate*, not eliminate those differences.

2. **Bring in success stories.** Sometimes connecting with at-risk students comes in the form of introducing them to *other* adults they can connect with — helping them build a team of positive role models to draw from.

    Make sure that you and your colleagues are not the only examples of "success" that your at-risk students have ever met. Make the effort to bring in community members, who look and speak like your students, but who have attained a level of success that they are proud of.

    Remember, I always tell my students: YOU define what success is, not the television or magazines. (I even have a song about this on one of my *Rappin' Mathematician* albums!)

    Ask around for the names of alumni who are successful, and invite them in to speak with your classes. With video conferencing, you can even have them speak to your class directly from their office.

    Let the conversation be real and even painful, if necessary. Let them discuss their struggles, failures and success openly and honestly (within an appropriate framework, of course). Be sure to reinforce this by telling your students that when *they* become successful, you expect that they will come in and speak to the students who now sit in their desk.

3. **Tell them about yourself.** Sometimes, it's hard to get at-risk students to open up and talk. Often, it's just not going to happen at all. But just because your students aren't talking, doesn't mean they're not listening.

Think about a funny story from your life (even better if it happened to you during the age of the students you're teaching). Pull a struggling student aside and tell her the story. Don't expect her to laugh. Just tell it with pride and confidence, and finish with, "I thought you might like to hear that story," and leave it at that.

Our most challenging students need to know that we are real people, who struggle, who ponder, and above all, who care.

Get to know your students by giving them a chance to get to know *you*.

So, the next time you find yourself intimidated or frustrated by a student who seems "checked out," unmotivated or unreachable, take a deep breath and remember Coach D — or some student of yours who "climbed out of the gap."

And remember that the key for these kids' turnarounds, from uninterested students to motivated and successful citizens, usually begins with a teacher or other adult who simply forms a relationship with them, and shows them that they care about them as people, their dreams and their success in life.

As Theodore Roosevelt famously said, "No one cares how much you know, until they know how much you care."

11

BEYOND THE "BAD KID"...

SENSIBLE STRATEGIES FOR BEHAVIOR MANAGEMENT WITH STRUGGLING STUDENTS

(co-authored with Pete Fisher)*

A student who is a chronic behavior problem can sink your whole class. All the detentions in the world don't seem to make a difference. Every phone call home seems to end with a no-answer, or a parent who is equally frustrated with the student. It's tempting to peg that student as the "bad kid."

Yet, as teachers, we are still the ones responsible for that student's learning, and the learning of his or her entire class. And we can't afford to see any kid as "bad" or beyond learning.

Especially working with at-risk or struggling students, we find ourselves needing to teach much more than the academic content in our books. As many of our students battle poverty, racism and a widening achievement gap, we're often the first ones to see the manifestations of these factors, in the ways these students act in class.

Furthermore, these behavioral manifestations often make it difficult, if not nearly impossible, to teach the planned lesson. Dealing with behavior is critical to our success in teaching at-risk or struggling students in any classroom.

If you're determined not to spend the rest of the school year disciplining the same student(s) with the same results (or lack thereof), it's time to take a deeper look at what is *behind* your students' disruptive behavior, and then enact some sensible strategies to handle it.

LOOKING BEHIND THE BEHAVIOR

To begin with, it is important to understand *why* a student would act out in class. We must understand that behaviors serve a function for an individual. A baby might scream and tantrum for a bottle of food when hungry. An elementary student might hit another child as a form of affection. A teenager might use profanity to gain peer acceptance and belonging.

All behaviors serve a function for an individual, and the form the behavior takes is actually a *process of communication*. In each example above, the behaviors were displayed because the child or teen did not know any alternative methods to get his or her needs met.

We must also remember that for some time the behavior has been rewarded in one way or another. The negative behavior is *working* for them; they are communicating and someone is paying attention.

If we remember this concept, we can start to shift behaviors. We can get to know our students as well as reasonably possible, and use our own life experiences along with some common-sense strategies to help us figure out what they may be trying to communicate — what they are really needing — and begin from there.

TURNING TROUBLE INTO SUCCESS

We all know from experience that there are sometimes obvious explanations for a student acting out, which we may be fortunate enough to learn in parent-counselor-teacher meetings — a breakup of a family, a violent situation, intense peer pressure, the loss of a home, a death in a student's life. When we know about these situations, we can work with a student to help fill their specific needs, which often changes behavior in class.

Other times, we aren't lucky enough to get a clear picture of what is going on with a student who is causing disruptive or destructive actions. When this is the case, we can still fall back on general tactics to help modify classroom misbehavior, even if we do not know the specific root of it for a student.

Here are five sensible strategies — which build on one another — to deal with negative, unwanted behaviors in your classroom and meet your students' needs:

1. **Remember what control really means.** It's often said that the only control we have over another person is that which the person will give us. As teachers, we can try to persuade our students to make good moral choices, but we can't physically force them into it.

    We can compel our students to make the right choices with encouragement, environment and incentives. Beyond that, we are only responsible for our own actions. Maintaining our own self-control and professionalism ensures the safety and welfare of the children we serve, and lets us be appropriate role models.

    Instead of trying to control students' behavior, then, we must always focus on controlling our own actions and on making our classroom into a place that encourages students to emulate constructive conduct.

2. **Create an environment where positive behaviors will likely occur.** So, the next step is observing our own classrooms and reflecting on whether or not their environments are conducive to every student's effective learning and communication.

    Does your classroom setup pay close attention to space: noise, temperature, light? Does your teaching offer a positive cadence, predictable structure, room for exploration and expression, and a sense of safety? What changes can you make to create this kind of environment for students?

Remember, factors in the environment usually trigger behaviors. If we can limit the number of triggers, chances are the potential for negative behaviors will be less likely to happen.

3. **Offer clear alternatives to negative behaviors.** As teachers in the pressure-cooker culture of many low-performing schools, we are often encouraged to focus on the academic curriculum without putting much emphasis on social skills building. Yet, many of our students do not have appropriate anger management, conflict resolution, or negotiation skills to solve challenges in communication, which stands in the way of learning.

Just like in academics, students need direct teaching, modeling, role-playing, practice and coaching of behavior skills. We cannot take for granted, at any age, that students are proficient at these skills.

Thus, we must come up with ways to model and communicate to students their alternatives to acting out. These can be anything from specific phrases to use when speaking or disagreeing to a cooling-off or meditation corner for anyone who needs a time-out.

These alternatives must be communicated verbally and visually in your classrooms, and practiced and reinforced. Unless we offer them real and specific alternatives, students will just continue with behaviors they know already.

4. **Think further about incentives.** Remember, students enact behaviors to get a need met, to protest an activity, or to avoid some type of aversive. Students have used certain behaviors that work for them, which eventually strengthen as a reward. We need to find incentives that are more powerful than what compels them to act out.

This means a lot more than candy bars or class parties. It means asking yourself how you can motivate your students *from within* to behave in new ways. To do this effectively, go back to looking at what they need and aren't getting.

Your incentive will somehow help fill this need. *Is it attention they need — how about a class talent contest every Friday after the lesson if they behave well all week? Is it stress release — how about organizing a "primal scream" for one full minute before testing day for the school?*

The possibilities are endless, but the point is focusing on filling their deeper needs as a true incentive for positive actions.

5. **Work together, and have a school plan.** The idea of an entire school being involved in meeting students' needs in ways that encourage positive behavior is a crucial concept for success with at-risk students. Student behavior problems always manifest beyond just one particular classroom.

   It's of course important for each teacher to enact her own classroom strategies, but it is *as important* that the larger school community is proactively dealing with behavior issues as well. Thus, all staff members working with at-risk students must work together to create a cohesive plan for dealing with escalating behaviors.

   The plan needs to include:
   - strategies to prevent escalation,
   - structured choice,
   - cooling-off or debriefing areas, and
   - possible consequences and specific conditions for these.

   The plan needs to be reviewed often and to evolve as the team grows and is challenged. Safety should always be the rule. Creative ideas (e.g., school assemblies) should be encouraged.

If there is not someone on staff already enacting this kind of broader procedure, suggest bringing in a behavior specialist — available through many school-district offices — to work with your team and put a plan in place.

In conclusion, we've all dealt with the "bad kid" who can drag our whole class down. But we also know, as teachers of at-risk and struggling students, that there are often severe and heartbreaking circumstances that may be causing a student to act badly.

Whether or not we can find out the specifics of each student's situation, it's our responsibility and our duty to look beyond the "bad kid" at what needs his behavior is communicating, and to continually enact strategies to meet those needs.

When we do this, we can effectively teach positive ways to communicate and behave, and make a tremendous difference in both the life of that student and in the learning of our entire class.

Pete Fisher is a former Behavior Specialist and 2006 Teacher of the Year for Escondido Union School District in California. He is a five-year standing cadre member of Southern California's Positive Environment of Network Trainers (PENT) and a trainer of Crisis De-escalation and Crisis Control.

12

"no, no, no!" OR QUID PRO QUO?

HOW TO negotiate WITH OUR at-RISK and STRUGGLING STUDENTS

Think about the best negotiator you know. Is it a businessperson who can close any deal? A lawyer who knows how to convince a skeptical jury? Or perhaps it's a kid who always seems to end up with the front seat in the car or the last cookie in the jar.

Whoever it is, I'll bet they enjoy the art of negotiation that moves people forward.

As teachers of at-risk or struggling students, it is crucial that we also embrace this art of negotiating and moving people forward — as a matter of survival. We also know that in a full classroom of high-need students, negotiations can become unclear, confusing and sometimes downright messy — and getting mired in them can stall the learning at stake for everyone.

We must understand how to negotiate efficiently and successfully in our classrooms, keeping up momentum with our students. Doing so allows us to get to teaching the content *they* need to understand for success in school and life.

THE FIRST GOAL: FINDING COMMON GROUND

The stalls we face with messy negotiations usually come down to one problem: *misaligned objectives.*

While a teacher's objective may be to have the students calculate the Pythagorean Theorem, identify an alliteration, or name all of the parts of an atom, an at-risk or struggling student's objective for the class could be something quite different. It may range from an attention-seeking desire to disrupt class, to simply staying awake.

Try as we might, we probably can't convince our students to see that we all should have the same objective in school — learning. But we need not let misaligned objectives stop us from helping learning happen.

To overcome opposing objectives, use successful negotiators' first important strategy for success: *finding common ground.*

To do this, shift your focus from the student's objective (say, to disrupt the class) to her need (perhaps, some attention). Observe a student off task and ask yourself, *what does she need?* Perhaps it is just some acknowledgement, or a safe space, or a way to let off some steam.

These needs are easy to meet — offer an encouraging comment, or a one-minute foot-stomping break. Once you have shown your student that you understand her need, you have placed yourself on common ground, in the optimal position for successfully negotiating with her to return to the lesson at hand.

FOUR STRATEGIES FOR SUCCESS

Beyond this common ground, you can use any number of approaches to move your students back to task. Here are four concepts, and examples, to keep in mind as you practice fine-tuning your classroom negotiation skills:

1. ***Reciprocity.*** One of the most obvious of negotiation strategies, reciprocity, relies on the principle of "Do this for me, and I'll do this for you." While it is often the simplest and quickest way to resolve a conflict, it can also result in creating a climate of expectations in which a struggling student will only work when given something in return.

Counteract this by using reciprocity in the context of *building on the student-teacher relationship*, and *building on the student's ultimate goals*. Start with reciprocity that is small and immediate, but grows into something that is long-term, and more gratifying, for the student.

For example, I had a student named Luis who always fell asleep in class. One day, we struck a deal that if he could just stay awake for an entire class period, he would earn a "front-of-the-lunch-line" pass.

After two days, we agreed that since this was becoming easy for Luis — and he was getting something positive out of being present in class — he now needed to stay awake for three consecutive days in order to earn the pass. However, since he was now accomplishing more, I offered more as well: at the end of the new three-day goal, he also earned 10 minutes on the computer playing the "multiplication blaster" video game.

In all honesty, Luis still fell asleep on occasion; however, it was no longer a daily event, and whenever this happened, we started his three-day cycle over. By then, we had built on the relationship enough so that when I enacted our agreement, he accepted it easily.

2. **Consistency.** Students are often off task not because they don't want to be participating in the class activity, but because *they are unclear as to what is expected of them.* Many of our at-risk students lack consistency in their personal lives and at home. Many have parents who are constantly working, and our students must fend for themselves when it comes to food, homework, and bedtime. Often, school is the only place that is a constant in their lives.

Thus, it is crucial that your *classroom routines, procedures and expectations* are consistent. This not only helps your students learn, it helps you avoid the constant and unsuccessful messiness of negotiating with them about what they should be doing at any given time.

If you use consistency, when one of your students is off task, you need remind him only of the *procedure* that he is not following, and do not need to get into a discussion about his behavior. This will save you much needed time and energy (not to mention your voice!) throughout the day.

If you haven't read Dr. Harry K. Wong's seminal book on classroom procedures, *The First Days of School,* run out and get it immediately. It is a truly fantastic guide to designing, implementing and enforcing consistency in your classroom.

3. *Social Validation.* I remember growing up as a kid, and the McDonald's near my house displayed the famous sign: "Over 1 million served." As we all know, that sign soon came to say, "Over 1 *billion* served." Each time I see that sign, I have an uncanny urge to go back to my meat-eating days, drive over and order a Big Mac. Why? Because if so many others are enjoying themselves at McDonald's, I should too, right?!

And how about the commercials for the latest pharmaceutical drug, which state, "Ask your doctor about xx, and join millions of others who have found relief..." Whether we like it or not, there is something to this classic "bandwagon" advertising principle that allows us to feel connected to others and part of a larger group.

As teachers, we can use this principle to guide the actions and outcomes of our students in a positive direction.

Sometimes, a new student comes into my class in the middle of the year, often because they have just been kicked out of their last school. Immediately upon guiding them to their assigned seat, I publicly welcome them into my classroom, and after introducing the new student, I ask the class to give them the "Two-Clap Welcome" (two claps in unison, followed by everyone shouting "Welcome!" together). I then assertively say, "This is a great class and you will enjoy being here. Everyone knows *exactly* what they need to be doing at all times!"

Not only does this reinforce the consistent routines in my class, it also sends a clear message that if you want social validation in my class, you'd better be doing what everyone else is.

Sometimes, when a student is off task, I'll simply walk over to them and quietly whisper, "Look around at your classmates. Every single one of them is working except for you. I need you to be productive like everyone else."

4. **Scarcity.** When you're at the store, and you see that there's only one bag of your favorite cookies left, do you grab it a bit more quickly than you normally would? Of course you do. If you don't, someone else might grab it, and you'll be left with nothing.

When you order something from the Internet, the first thing you want to know is "How quickly can I get it?" Although you've lived your entire life without it, suddenly you need it now.

Scarcity of resources, and scarcity of time, gets us to act quickly. Utilize this knowledge in your classroom.

When practicing a math problem, I'll sometimes say, "You have exactly 2 minutes and 30 seconds to complete this problem." Rarely will any students ever stop to ask, "Or what?" They're too busy working. If they do, I simply reply, "Now you've only got 2 minutes and 10 seconds."

At the end of class, to gain closure on the lesson, I'll often utilize "exit tickets," where the students have to complete a problem on a small scrap of paper in order to leave the classroom. If they don't act quickly, they don't get to leave the classroom on time. Or I'll say, "Only the first 10 people who get the correct answer get to leave on time."

Once, after holding a student an extra minute after lunch began, he said sadly, "Now all the good food will be gone, I'll have to eat the chicken nuggets." *Exactly*, I thought to myself. (And, ugh, can we please talk about school lunches?!)

From scarcity of time, to scarcity of cafeteria food, use this negotiation tactic to keep your students moving.

Negotiating with a struggling student can be a daunting task. Negotiating with a room full of them can be downright intimidating. However, view these negotiations with creativity, fairness and the above four tactics, and you'll find that you can turn even the most unwilling student into one that is on board and on task, and your classroom into one that consistently moves forward in the direction of learning.

13

HOW TO HOOK THE UNINVOLVED PARENT

THREE BASIC STRATEGIES AND CAN'T-MISS IDEAS TO REEL PARENTS IN

In Your Classroom

As teachers in low-performing schools, we've all had the exact same experience, many times over, when calling the parents of some of our at-risk students.

It goes something like this:

> Ring, ring…
> Ring, ring…
> Ring, ring…
> Ring, ring…
> Ring, ring…
> *(hang up phone)*

If we are lucky enough to catch a parent, we're often greeted by a less-than-enthusiastic person who seems uninterested in improving their child's behavior or academic performance. Convincing them to come onto our campus to meet with teachers is harder than the gum under our students' desks.

However, we can't give up. Getting parents (or guardians) invested in their children's education is a critical factor in reaching struggling and at-risk students, and in helping them to succeed.

Connect with an uninvolved parent, and you can potentially turn your most challenging student into a valuable part of your classroom culture.

To be clear: yes, I do believe it is a part of our job as teachers of at-risk students to help bridge the gaps in their families as well as their classrooms. So, my strategy is to get creative and get to work.

Here are three strategies I use to try to "hook" the uninvolved parent:

1. **Remember: technology is your friend.** I must admit, I was a little offended last week when, five days after I left a message for a friend, he hadn't returned my call, but I noticed that he had been very active on his Facebook page. However, instead of dwelling on the fact that he was able to spend so much time chatting online but not call me back, I simply left him a short message on his Facebook page. He responded to me immediately.

   We now live in a fast-paced, up-to-the-minute, technology-driven world, where communication happens online, in real-time, and consists of two sentences or less. Why not apply these principles to getting parents involved?

   Get a parent's cell phone number, and offer to send them a text message update of their child's performance. It could be as simple as "Miguel was off-task today, please speak with him when you see him." Or "Valerie just got an A on her math quiz." Consider sending the text message while the student is right in front of you.

   Perhaps this will not get the parent into the school for a meeting, but it will certainly keep them more involved. When you do get the parent to agree to come onto campus, be sure to send them a "text message reminder" an hour or so before the meeting.

   Also, consider starting an on-line class forum, such as a Facebook page, blog, or teacher website. Most forums take mere minutes to set up, and parents will be able to sign up, sign in, and get involved as often as they want.

It will also allow them to leave comments, or check what homework has been assigned. Many forums can now be linked to the district website where grades can be immediately accessed by the parents!

2. **Offer free food and childcare.** Let's be honest here, what would you rather go to: a free meeting, or a free meal?

When inviting a parent in to discuss their child's issues, mention that you'll have coffee and muffins, popcorn and fruit, or whatever — and let them know that you'll have enough for the siblings as well.

If you're lucky, the parent might even show up with some food to share. Working in a predominantly Latino neighborhood, I've enjoyed eating more than a few delicious *pupusas* as the result of a parent meeting.

On the sibling note, we all know how frustrating it can be to try to conduct a parent meeting while younger siblings are running around (or out of) the classroom. Plus, I often feel very badly when having an honest conversation with a parent and student, and a younger brother or sister (who usually looks up to their older sibling) is sitting there listening to less than stellar things being said about the student.

Consider teaming up with another teacher not involved in the meeting, and set them in a corner of the room with some age-appropriate books, supervised games, or activities that the younger siblings can participate in while the conference is taking place. It might require you to repay that teacher with 20 minutes of your time later; however, we all know that getting an at-risk student on track pays for itself in the classroom management department!

3. **Think like a salesperson.** A good friend of mine is a toy salesman. Part of his job includes cold-calling toy stores to make appointments with store managers to come by and show them the latest products. The problem? He found it very difficult to get in touch with any of them.

So, after leaving a message with his name and number, he began saying, "Tell xx I'll call him back at 3:30 this afternoon." Sure enough, when he called back at the specified time, he suddenly found that many managers were *expecting* his call.

When leaving a message for a parent, try simply telling them that you'll call back at 7:30 p.m. tonight (and be sure to call at that time!). Not only does it take the pressure off the parent to call back, it unofficially makes both you and the parent accountable for the communication.

Then, when you begin the conversation, *start with something nice.*

When my friend the toy salesman begins conversations with commenting on how happy everyone in the store seems, or how clean the floors are, the store mangers are much more likely to feel comfortable and relaxed. Don't our students' parents deserve the same?

Many parents of at-risk students have been experiencing phone calls from teachers for years now, telling them how badly behaved their children are, or how they never do their homework. Consider starting the conversation by complimenting something the student has done recently (even if you have to dig deep into yourself to find something!). This will not only help to establish rapport with the parent, but it might just encourage them to pick up the phone the next time you call!

In conclusion, hooking an uninvolved parent can be a frustrating hassle. One of my colleagues recently referred to it as "trying to chase a mouse around the house with a spoon." However, with creativity, technology and some free cheese, we might soon find ourselves holding that mouse by the tail.

14

STUDENT-LED CONFERENCES

SEVEN STEPS TO EMPOWERING OUR STUDENTS BY PUTTING THEM IN CHARGE

*(co-authored with Mindy Crum)**

When I was a kid, I loved going to my parent-teacher conferences. I remember sitting around my teacher's desk with my mom and teacher, early in the morning before the school day began, eagerly awaiting the grown-up conversation.

Of course, I attended school in a middle-class neighborhood in a solid school district, and my mom was very involved in my education. As I consistently earned good grades, I often left the conferences beaming with pride at all the nice things my teachers said about me.

Unfortunately, this is not the reality for many students, especially at-risk ones.

For these students, parent-teacher conferences are a half-hour (or more) of teachers telling their parents or guardians how many homework assignments they haven't completed, how poor their scores were on the latest round of standardized tests, and how they need to modify and improve their behavior. That is, assuming the parents even show up at all.

This format and experience — of teachers talking at parents while the student sits idly by — only further discourages already-challenged students and rarely leads to improvement.

a new kind of conference

Instead, I offer you another option — a way to make teacher conferences an opportunity for at-risk and struggling students to engage and walk away feeling empowered, rather than dejected. The *student-led conference* allows all students to take an active role in their own learning and development.

Not only does it give them a leadership role (something often lacking in traditional schooling of at-risk students), it also gives them the ability to prepare data, present information and answer questions — all real-life skills that are critical to academic and career success.

I've found student-led conferences to be a revelation for my at-risk students, as has Mindy Crum, an experienced teacher of this population of students, whom I asked to co-author this column. After implementing student-led conferences at our low-performing schools, we both experienced a positive shift in students' attitudes before, during and after parent conferences.

seven steps to student-led conferences

Below are seven steps you can take to have your students run their own conferences this year, and give them an opportunity to think critically, speak articulately, and own their learning:

> **Step 1: Select and Announce Dates.** Selecting and announcing conference dates at the beginning of the school year secures your commitment to running your conferences differently this year. It also gives the students time to process that they will really be conducting their own conferences this year, and gives them a timeline of how much they'll need to prepare.
>
> Perhaps your school site or district already has prearranged days for parent conferences, often only once per school year. If so, we suggest adding a second conference period

during the school year, and even a third, year-end conference period, to give students and parents maximum benefit from this format.

While this does take some extra planning and practice, once the structure is in place, we have found that conferences (and the time between conferences) become a pleasure, as the students engage and improve more each time. The third conference can be used to close out the school year, in celebration of reaching goals, working through challenges, or simply to reflect on learning that has taken place.

Mindy also found that she is able to save time by scheduling more than one parent conference at the same time. Since most of the talking is done by the students themselves, she can bounce around the room, and sit in on conferences that are occurring simultaneously (see "Step 7" for more details).

Step 2: Ongoing Communication. Communicating with parents is essential for successful student-led conferences. Be sure to notify parents several weeks prior to the conference week that you will be setting up student-led conferences where both the child and parent need to attend.

Make it clear to parents that *their child* will be running the conference, and what an exciting opportunity this is to see their child "in action." This often takes the pressure off of parents, especially those who are English language learners, and makes them more likely to come.

Make sure to offer a wide range of conference times to ensure that parents can attend at their scheduled time. Place the responsibility on the students for getting their parent(s) there, and teach them "reminder tools," such as writing it on the calendar at home, leaving written reminders on the refrigerator (or other high-traffic area in the home), or sending reminder texts/emails to reinforce the importance of attendance. When sending letters home, be sure that they are written in the parents' native language.

Step 3: Students Gather Data. Just as an effective sales presentation would include relevant data, any student conference should as well. Give students a clear picture of what information they will be responsible for sharing during their conference (attendance, grades, standardized test scores, etc.). Help them understand the data they will be presenting, why it is important, and how to effectively showcase it.

Prior to the actual conference, have students spend time analyzing the data, perhaps comparing it with other students (a built-in math lesson!), and organizing it. This organization should also include other information that will be presented, such as goal binders, reading levels, recent test/homework scores, as well as a "big-picture" idea of how all aspects fit together.

Step 4: Students Complete Checklist. After the data has been gathered and organized, students need to complete a checklist. Not only does this checklist ensure that the students are well-prepared and thorough, it can also serve as a guide for use *during* the conference. Mindy includes a list of items the students are to share with their parents (such as homework and reading logs), test scores, semester goals, and the student's leadership role in the class.

You can create your checklist any way that works for the data your students will share with their parents. Make sure not to leave anything to the last minute — have students complete the checklist at least a week prior to the conference, as well as have their needed materials ready (data notebooks, test scores, writing samples, etc.). This helps them feel relaxed, and also invested in getting their parents to the conference to see the work they have prepared.

Step 5: The Dress Rehearsal. Like any good presenter, students need time to practice; and for many, running a meeting will be a new experience. This practice is most effective (and fun) when done with another adult acting as the parent.

Recruit your principal, librarian, nurse, on-campus adult volunteers, and other teachers who are considering incorporating student-led conferences into their own pedagogy. Model first to students how to share their data, using the checklist as a guide, if necessary. Explain to the "stand-in" adults that their role is to be a listening guide, and to ask clarifying questions as necessary.

Important: make the practice authentic to the situation students will face at the real conference. Set up stations in the room where the conferences will be held.

If students will be speaking primarily in a language other than English, have them practice in that language as well. A student whose parents speak only Spanish should not have to translate their words for the first time in front of their parents. If the actual conference is scheduled for 15 minutes, have students practice for the equivalent amount of time.

If you are not able to recruit adults, you can always pair up students, taking turns in the roles of "student" and "parent," or ask students from higher grades to fill in.

Step 6: Room Set-up. The set-up of the room is extremely important, especially if you have several conferences occurring at once. As many parents (especially those who do not speak English well, or who come from a different culture) are often intimidated or uncomfortable in a school, be sure to create a warm and welcoming environment.

Playing quiet classical music is very helpful in both creating a relaxed atmosphere and preventing simultaneous conversations from being overheard. Have the student data and checklists easily accessible at the entrance of the classroom, such as in a folder in a file box, placed on a desk at the entrance.

When setting up conference stations, we recommend placing two desks next to each other with four chairs (for student, parent, teacher and interpreter, if needed). Set up the conference stations in the corners of the room, which creates maximum spacing between groups for privacy. It is also a good idea to have the child and parent sit next to each other (not across from each other), so that both can read what is being presented.

Step 7: The Conference. As you talk up the conferences in the week prior, students will become both anxious and excited. Take this opportunity to explain to them that these are normal emotions, but keep them focused on the goal of running a productive conference that will result in the development of their speaking and leadership skills.

Trust that they will become empowered through the process of sharing, discussing, and understanding their own learning by articulating it to their parents.

As the conferences get underway, float from one conference to another (if you have chosen to schedule more than one at the same time), making sure to double-check that students are using the checklist correctly. Of course, anticipate that some students will need you to be physically seated there for the entire conference, and schedule and plan accordingly.

Finally, find a way to close the conference in a way that is positive and action-driven.

Consider ending the conference with the child, parent and teacher signing the conference checklist where "New Goals" had been written. Be sure to copy the checklist, and send it home as soon after the conference as possible.

ARE STUDENT-LED CONFERENCES WORTH THE EFFORT?

Our answer: unequivocally, *Yes!* We found that students', parents' and our own experience of conference time was transformed for the better when we implemented student-led conferences. Although it requires more effort and organization up front, we found conference time to be "easier" and much more rewarding this way.

By taking responsibility for clearly communicating their own progress and goal-setting, students improve not only their learning engagement and confidence, but their oral language skills as well. And we've watched with joy as parents listen intently to their child's sharing of successes and struggles, which can serve to strengthening the lines of communication between them.

Great conferences needn't be a rarity for at-risk students. Student-led conferences offer them an opportunity to not just survive in the academic world, but to take an empowering leadership role in it.

* *Mindy Crum is a fourth-grade teacher at a Title 1 school in North San Diego County, where the majority of her students are second language learners who live in shared housing. Ms. Crum has taught first, third and fourth graders for over a decade.*

PART TWO

TeaCHeR as COLLeague

*Strategies for Succeeding
as a Member of a Staff Team*

15

MAKING MEETINGS AN HOUR TO EMPOWER

STRATEGIES FOR TURNING "NOT ANOTHER MEETING!" INTO "LET'S GET TO BUSINESS!"

As teachers today, we have a lot on our plates. As a result, we have a lot to discuss — and that discussion usually takes place in the form of a meeting. The problem? There's a meeting every day (at least!).

From IEPs (Individualized Education Plans), to BSPs (Behavior Support Plans), our PLC (Professional Learning Community) seems to hold more meetings than there are education acronyms. And when it comes to meetings about our students, especially students in crisis, there is a lot at stake in each discussion.

We don't have time to waste in long and unproductive meetings. At the same time, meetings are critical for keeping schools and teaching teams functioning. Communication and collaboration are imperative for helping our students.

Devalue a meeting, and we simultaneously devalue a chance to make a collective difference in the lives of those who need us most.

So how can we make our meetings efficient and productive? There are of course the stand-by rules of starting on time, keeping discussions on topic, etc. Beyond that, though, it is imperative that every teacher and staff member leave each meeting feeling focused and empowered.

Here are four tips to accomplish a deeper level of empowerment and productivity in your meetings:

1. **Reward creative thought.** As teachers, we are not only teaching for the world as it is, but for the world *as it can be.* New ideas are critical to our success.

   Consider (as a tradition) giving out a "Creative Thinker of the Trimester" award to the meeting attendee who has come up with the most important new ideas, or who has been instrumental in seeing a new idea come to fruition. This award sends out a clear message: We are holding these meetings in order to evolve as a group.

   This evolution happens through creativity, not just standard discussion about the "same old issues." In addition, the opportunity to bring in a fresh idea will get people thinking about new ideas when they are away from the meetings — a sure sign that the meetings are productive!

2. **Invite "special guests" from time to time.** Let's be honest — when you know in advance that another professional is coming in to observe you teaching, don't you try harder? Perhaps you tidy up the room a bit beforehand, or dress a little nicer that day. As teachers, we are proud of our work, and we love to "show it off" a bit. The same concept can apply in meetings.

   When regularly scheduled meetings begin to feel a bit mundane, invite in a "special guest." Perhaps another teacher from another subject or grade level. Perhaps someone who is not normally invited to these types of meetings, such as one of the clerical staff or an instructional aid. Not only will the normal participants want to "show off their work" a bit, they will hopefully do it in a manner that is organized and professional.

Inviting the occasional guest is also a great reminder that the decisions made (and carried out) affect more than just those who attend the meetings — they have potentially a larger-scale effect on the entire school community. And those invited will often come enthusiastic to attend and contribute, and will return to their own department meetings full of fresh ideas and perspective.

3. **Turn "routines" into "traditions."** What's the difference between a "routine" and a "tradition?" A *routine* is something that we do repeatedly, either consciously or subconsciously. A *tradition* is something special that we choose to do, often to celebrate an aspect of our culture. With "traditions," a sense of family develops, and even the most mundane can become important and cherished.

    Stop and consider how you can make this shift in thinking in your own group. Can you add a prop or ritual to something seemingly dull — like weekly check-ins or student progress reports — to bring either some levity or deeper meaning? Can you come up with a team cheer? Make one meeting a month a "bring breakfast" meeting during which you take 20 minutes to share your successes?

    It may sound trivial, but creating traditions brings people together, encourages them to feel connected, and reminds them of why they do what they do.

4. **Take the vision off the wall, and put it on the table.** All too often, we put items on our meeting agendas because we have to. Perhaps an administrator told us to discuss something and report back. Perhaps it's a piece of business that just needs to get done.

    As teachers, we know that telling our students they need to learn something "because we said so," or "because it will be on the test," is a sure-fire way to have them become immediately disengaged. Our students want to know *why* they need the information we are teaching. They need to know how it will help them in their daily activities, and throughout their lives.

Shouldn't the same principles apply in our meetings?

Consider expanding the traditional roles of "facilitator and recorder," and assigning the role of "process observer" at your meetings. Someone whose role it is to state *why* it is the meeting is happening in the first place, and to later determine whether the original goals of the meeting were accomplished.

In addition, the process observer can comment on the overall tone of the meeting, and highlight any significant thought that has resulted. Having this person end by reminding everyone of something positive that occurred is also a great way to close the meeting with everyone feeling good about the time they've just spent, and excited to get back into their classrooms.

We're always going to have full plates as teachers, and we're always going to have meetings.

As professionals, we hold meetings to exchange ideas, disseminate information, and create a culture of collaboration within our organization. As educators, we embody the commitment inherent to our role, by inspiring in our students the pride and confidence to make this world a better place.

With effective, innovative, positive and productive meetings, aimed ultimately at helping our students — we're doing all this together.

16

welcome to teaching. please stay.

HOW TO HELP YOUR SCHOOL'S new teachers succeed (and stick around)

Brenda was one of the most promising new teachers our school had ever seen — her student teaching with at-risk students got glowing reviews, she was eager to jump right into leadership roles, and her classroom was well-organized and ready days before veteran teachers had even set foot on campus.

Weeks into her first teaching year, though, she pulled me aside to tell me she felt that the staff did not want to connect with her. One colleague had even told her there was no point investing time into first-year teachers, since most of them left. "Once you show up for your second year, you'll be treated like you belong here," Brenda had been told.

We've all heard the dismal teacher turnover numbers, such as the National Education Association's (NEA) calculation that 20% of teachers in urban schools leave each year, a large majority still just in their first three years in the profession. And we know the consequences: beyond the cost of replacing each teacher who leaves (which is estimated anywhere from $15,000 to $40,000), there is also the toll on staff morale, student confidence, and test scores.

It is imperative that we teachers look at our own personal responsibility in these statistics. Let's ask ourselves: *Am I doing all I can to help new teachers at my school succeed? Or am I contributing to their departure by ignoring or belittling them?*

At Your School

Imagine the positive effect could we have on our schools — and ultimately the success of our students — if each of us made it a personal goal to help our schools' new teachers feel welcome, invest in the job, and stay on board.

FOUR STRATEGIES FOR encouraging new TeaCHeRS

Thinking there may be more you can do to welcome and encourage new teachers? Here are a few easy ways to start:

1. **Minimize negative talk.** I still remember the uncomfortable, embarrassed feeling I had when I was sitting in the teacher's lounge my first year and a group of veteran teachers began to lambaste the district BTSA (New Teacher Induction) program. One by one, they fired off a round of cynical comments about the program's uselessness.

   I actually had been loving the program, felt I was learning a lot, and had wanted to share some of the insights from our latest BTSA guest speaker at the next staff meeting. (Guess whether I did after that teacher's lounge experience.)

   I know, schools have a lot of issues, and the longer we staff members are there the more familiar we are with those issues, and the more likely we are to complain about them. But, let's try to refrain from badmouthing the administration, fellow teachers, programs, and students in front of new teachers.

   This doesn't mean being fake or keeping new teachers out of the loop — but give them a chance to be excited, bring a fresh energy to the table, and form their own opinions before we impose our weathered ones.

   On the other hand, a little humor about the issues at your school can work wonders for a new teacher's perspective. Oh, the relief I felt my first semester when fellow teachers were joking about certain student behaviors I had assumed were happening only in my classroom!

In short, when it comes to the challenges of our profession, levity works much better than negativity for helping new teachers thrive.

2. **Celebrate milestones and successes.** Getting through the first week of school may not be a big deal to you now, but remember what an accomplishment it was your first year?

Take a few minutes to walk into your new teachers' classrooms and notice what they are doing. Acknowledge their seemingly small milestones — the first month, the first back-to-school night, the first parent conferences — and you not only help motivate them, but you open the door to asking them how things are going and if they need anything.

Call out new teachers' triumphs — high first test scores, calm handling of a student scuffle — in staff meetings as well. Consider making a ritual of celebrating one new teacher's accomplishment at each department or PLC meeting. You could even come up with a funny name for it: a "groovy newbie" award?

There's a larger reward in doing this as well. If you honor new teachers publicly for their successes, you not only boost their morale but you set an example of teamwork and support that they will likely emulate, adding a positive vibe to your staff meetings for years to come. By helping new teachers in encouraging ways through that tough first year, you are also helping your own experience as a staff member in the future.

3. **Include them in decision-making (but don't force it).** A few years ago my math department received a $400 grant and we didn't know what to spend it on. After we hemmed and hawed for a while, a new teacher spoke up

and described a teaching tool he had seen at a conference. It sounded amazing, we looked into it, and ultimately ended up using the grant to purchase it. I still remember the smile on the new teacher's face when we listened to his idea.

It's easy to blow off a new teacher who brings up an issue or question we've heard a million times before, and it's normal to struggle with taking seriously a colleague as old as your kids. But, try to remember when you were in those new teacher shoes and how much it meant (or would have meant) when you were included as a peer.

Before you roll your eyes at the neophytes, open your ears: they just may surprise you with a great idea or insight.

On the flip side, don't force new teachers into jobs they can't handle. We all know how tempting it is to throw first-year teachers to the wolves by sticking them with the worst volunteer or leadership duties. But, putting them in charge of the notoriously rowdy first dance is not a way to boost their confidence or help them survive their first year.

Let them get involved at their own pace, in duties that play to their strengths, which benefits everyone.

4. **Help them stay healthy.** The first month of my first year of teaching, each night I scarfed down a drive-through burrito for dinner after leaving school at 8 p.m.

Then, a fellow teacher invited me to join him for an after-school surf on Thursdays (San Diego's equivalent of the East Coast racquetball date). I began looking forward to our surf session all week, felt so much better the day of and after it, and saw that I was actually able to leave school in the daylight and take care of myself now and then.

I've seen dozens of new teachers work themselves into sickness from the pressure of that first year on the job.

Notice when your new teachers look unwell, mention headaches or stomachaches or have frequent doctor's appointments. Try to encourage them to give themselves a break and make their health a priority. Invite them on a weekend hike, offer them a guest pass to your gym, or bring them some fresh fruit from your backyard trees.

Show them that other teachers care about their health, and they can, too.

Sharing stories of how stressed out or sick you were your first year (I threw up before school those first few days and got three colds my second semester) can help them feel less alone. Sharing how well you feel now can help them see that things do get better (not even a sniffle last year, and I still try to hit the waves once a week).

Again, there's the personal picture and the big picture: by helping an individual teacher be healthier you also help your school. Well teachers mean less sick days taken, and better teaching in general, which is what our students, and our faculty teams, need.

I'm happy to report that Brenda — that promising new teacher — is now a thriving veteran teacher. She succeeded despite her first-year challenges with cynical and unsupportive colleagues. But many new teachers do not; they leave feeling alienated and we all pay the price.

Each one of us can make a difference this year by supporting the Brendas and all the new teachers at our school. Remember when you were in their shoes, and treat them as you wanted to be treated — when you entered this great profession to help students in great need of great teachers.

17

TALKING 'BOUT MY GENERATION!

STRATEGIES FOR IMPROVING TODAY'S SCHOOLS BY "MINDING THE GENERATION GAPS" AMONG TEACHERS

Recently, I was invited to give a presentation at one of our district's elementary schools about a new computerized assessment program. When I arrived at the school site, the principal told me, "My staff is comprised mostly of veteran teachers who are not very comfortable with computers. In fact, we can't even get some of them to check their email."

Sure enough, as I gave the presentation, I noticed the few young teachers quickly absorbing and applying the information, while the "veteran" teachers sat, arms-crossed, with a bewildered look on their faces. I left the site with a newly defined challenge before me: turning that "generation gap" into an asset for *all* teachers and students.

START TALKING...

Newsflash: We need to change the way we think, and talk, about the generation gaps among teachers.

While teaching is a profession that has us working shoulder-to-shoulder with colleagues across several generations, we often ignore this. Or we focus on the voids each generation brings to the table, rather than the strengths that can fill those voids.

These days, with the volatility of pink slips and uncertainty of budgets, there is often a division between long-standing teachers with many years in the same classroom, and newer teachers who have spent the past few years bouncing from job to job.

Like many issues of diversity, this is one we may find hard to talk about, and it might be easier to focus on what divides rather than what can bring together. But, what would happen if we actually discussed this issue head-on, and focused on what these groups of teachers can offer one another — rather than allow the generation gap to grow, which only hurts us *and* our students?

Here's what I know: When it comes to helping *one student*, nothing is more critical than the relationship between the teacher and the student. However, when it comes to helping *an entire school*, nothing is more critical than the relationships between the adults in the building.

Transforming teachers' generational differences into a staff's strength (one that can help generations of students) requires a real understanding of generational issues, and some creative solutions, which can be implemented at any site.

UNDERSTANDING THE GENERATIONS

While exact years may vary from report to report, there are generally four generations currently at work in our schools and offices — which is a first in American history, and can be an amazing opportunity for all of us. Simply naming these generational groups can begin to shed light on what we are dealing with.

So, in general, the four working generations are:

- **The Traditionalists:** Also known as "The Silent Generation," Traditionalists were born between 1925 and 1945, and were shaped by events such as The Great Depression and World War II.

- **The Baby Boomers:** Born between 1946 and 1964, and our nation's largest generation, the Baby Boomers were deeply affected by events such as the Vietnam War and the 1960's.

- **Generation X:** Born between 1965 and 1980, the Gen X'ers were shaped by events such as the explosion of the Challenger Space Shuttle, and the Iraq War.

- **The Millennials:** Also referred to as "Gen Y" or "Gen Next," the 80's-to-90's-born Millennials came of age with events such as the school shootings at Columbine, 9/11 and the advent of the internet, which has ushered us into the current "information age."

With such a wide range of years on our planet and the experiences that have generally shaped each generation's thinking (and thus, approach to teaching), it is critical that our schools take the steps necessary to not only bridge the gaps between the generations, but to use them as an advantage in improving our schools.

THRee STRaTeGIeS TO BRIDGe THe DIVIDe

The following strategies can get your staff started in talking about generational issues, and making the most of this kind of diversity on our teams.

1. **Acknowledge and celebrate generational differences openly.** Pretending that age and cultural differences do not exist will only widen the gap between generations. Naming and celebrating this range of perspectives on your staff can open doors to conversations and ideas that may never surface otherwise.

   There is plenty of fascinating research that delves into the generalized personality traits that come with each generational cohort, which can be helpful as you work on this issue in your school teams. As long as everyone agrees up front to be mindful of stereotyping, and understand that no one fits completely into these group traits, it can be a fun exercise to talk about the general strengths and challenges each generation brings to the table.

Consider having the staff all read a book on generations working together — such as *From Boomers to Bloggers: Success Strategies Across Generations* by Misti Burmeister — and have a discussion about it. You can also try using 15 minutes of three or four staff meetings (depending on the age span of your particular staff) to have each generational group offer up what they think their generational perspective can contribute to the team's success as a whole.

2. **Create teams, mentorships and communications that mind the gaps.** A lot of our systems as school staffs only widen the generational divide — one-way mentorships, teams that don't take generations into account, communications in only one mandated style.

Think about empowering *all* generations when rethinking these systems at your school or district.

For example, instead of setting up a system in which the veteran teachers get their pick of the classes they teach, and the newest teachers fill in the gaps, create a system based on equitable distribution of students and teaching assignments. Instead of simply pairing up new teachers with veteran teachers to have the veterans teach the newbies, make it a two-way mentorship, where each has something to teach the other.

And, instead of choosing only one way to communicate among staff, come up with creative ways to get information out that fits the different styles of the generations — perhaps even creating a cross-generational communication team, where one member texts, one emails, and one photocopies important announcements to various staff sub-groups, based on preference.

There is no need to force all generations to "conform" to some other generation's way of being. With a little innovative thinking and teamwork, there are plenty of ways to respect and acknowledge generational differences that can unite rather than divide.

3. **Remember the common goal.** Next time I walk into a mixed-generation group of teachers to talk about computerized testing, I will first be sure to acknowledge the gift of the generational span in the room — the veterans who may better understand and can tell us about the history and reasoning behind testing in our district, and the fresh teachers who can likely help us all feel more comfortable with the new techie nature of the beast.

   Perhaps I will pair them up, or lighten the mood by playing a little "generations game" (putting so-called traits of each generation on the board, having them pick which goes with which, then discussing how we need them all to implement this new system).

   Then, I will be sure to hit hard on what matters most to *all* of the generations of teachers in the room: *the success of our students.* Whether you are a seasoned teacher who has "seen it all," or a new teacher ready to change the world — we are all here because we believe in the promise of our *future generations.*

   It is our job to help our students learn and thrive, and to do this, we must pool all of our strengths and never lose sight of this shared and fundamental goal of the work we do.

An Issue That's Here To Stay

In closing, one important idea I learned from reading about generations is that our generational culture stays with us, so we will never truly "grow into" understanding or being like the generations before us. In other words, a Baby Boomer at 25 was very different than a Millennial at 25, and they will retain this difference at their respective age 50.

The same is true for the generational perspective of our students — their youthful selves are simply different than ours were, and they will never see the world as we do.

So, it behooves us to accept and celebrate that each generation brings something unique to the table that will remain as such, and working *with* these differences serves all of us — from our individual student relationships to the overall culture of our staffs, schools and districts.

Let's start talking 'bout *all* of our generations as we strive to come together as colleagues and serve students each day.

18

we need to Talk...

an 8-step strategy for approaching a colleague about a conflict

When I signed on to be a full-time coach for teachers, my district administrators told me I'd be designing professional development, conducting sample lessons, and helping teachers plan and assess curriculum.

While I do all these things daily, what strikes me most is how often I'm called in to help coach a teacher on approaching a colleague who is being "difficult."

As teachers, part of our job is to help students learn to get along — and yet I'm seeing how often teachers need lessons in managing conflict among ourselves.

The foundation of these lessons, I've found, is to look more deeply into the concept of conflict itself.

Rethinking conflict

Conflict is not always a negative. It can be a positive catalyst to push us into new growth. For any successful organization, conflict is inextricably linked to those turning points that lead to success.

Unfortunately, for an organization that is flailing, inability to deal with conflict is usually at the root of the problems. And for teachers, we can't afford to let our own inability to handle conflict negatively affect our focus on the critical job at hand — educating our students.

Our students come from many different walks of life, some entering our classrooms with the weight of the world on their shoulders. The last thing they need is a teacher who is distracted by "adult conflict" instead of focused on being the best teacher he can be.

In schools, conflict between two adults can build up over years, as some teachers stay at the same school site (even in the same classroom) for decades. However, with most schools placing an increased emphasis on collaboration and Professional Learning Communities (PLCs), many teachers are being drawn out of their own classrooms, and into meetings where communication often goes awry. This ends up leaving the adults angry, bewildered, and unsure how to approach their colleagues to resolve issues.

I see this changing dynamic, which pushes teachers to deal with their own conflicts, as *a great opportunity* for all of us.

The better we can become at handling challenging situations with one another, the better we can become at handling the challenging situations our students face. We also have the chance to truly "practice what we preach" in learning to get along with one another.

TaKING a POSITIVe APPROaCH

I actually greatly enjoy the "conflict coaching" I've been doing with teachers, as I love to see the light bulb turn on in teachers' eyes when they see how easy it can be to handle a troubling situation with a colleague. I've seen so much growth occur, among individuals and staff teams, when conflict is addressed productively and positively.

The following is a step-by-step approach that any teacher can use to approach a colleague in a way that is professional, respectful and ultimately beneficial for the relationship — and thus for the rest of the staff and students as well.

Step 1: Be well-rounded. Think about the situation from at least three different perspectives: yours, your colleague's, and the students'. Whatever the situation is that you need to confront, thinking about it from multiple perspectives will help you see the situation more fully, and will help you begin to pinpoint exactly what the issues are.

It can be quite helpful to write this down. You can write "What I Need," "What My Colleague Needs," and "What Students Need" as you analyze the situation.

This helps you clarify your own issues, put yourself in a position of empathy toward your colleague, and re-focus on the ultimate goal of best serving your students. It also helps you step away from the "drama" these situations often entail, and look at the situation more objectively.

Step 2: Confirm behavior without publicly criticizing. Often, we wonder if a colleague's behavior is bothering others, or if we're the only ones noticing.

It's OK to privately ask another colleague for her perspective; however, avoid going to her complaining or criticizing. Doing so will only push her to defend the person or criticize along with you. Either way, it places her in an uncomfortable position she did not ask for, and doesn't help the situation.

Instead, remain professional and upbeat, and focus on specific behavior and how it affects the group. Explain that you are asking not to gossip, but to help improve the situation for everyone.

For example, when approaching a colleague about another colleague who constantly interrupts and dominates the conversation during meetings, consider using one of the following line(s):

"I really want to approach Linda about the way she behaves in meetings, as I'm concerned that it's affecting our faculty morale and productivity. However, first I wanted to check with you to see what your perspective is on the situation."

"I'm concerned about Linda's behavior in meetings, and how it may be affecting the group. Have you or anyone on the team ever approached her about this?"

Be sure to really listen for insights you can glean — not just to validate your perspective, but also to challenge or open it up. After hearing your colleague's input, politely end the conversation, and let her know that you will inform her of what you decide to do.

Step 3: Make an appointment. It is important that this conversation takes place in a comfortable, private location, with plenty of time to have it. Catching someone off guard is not only unfair, it often blocks the ability to have a conversation that is relaxed and real. This is especially true if someone needs to rush off, or was planning on doing something else.

Here are two ideas for making an appointment:

1) Stop into your colleague's classroom right before a class begins, and say, "Hey, I was hoping to talk to you, but I know class is about to begin. When would be a good time? How about right after school (or at break, lunch, etc.) today?"

    This will give your colleague plenty of advance notice, which he had a decision in, and will signal him that a conversation is coming. This can also be emailed in advance if you aren't able to get to his class/office.

2) In the event that the conversation needs to happen now, you can still begin the conversation by saying, "Hey, I need to talk to you. Is now a good time?" If it is not a good time, trust that he will let you know.

Otherwise, when he agrees that now *is* a good time, he has a moment to collect himself, and at least has had a say in the meeting taking place at that moment.

Step 4: Rehearse and open with confidence. When you approach a colleague about a conflict, it's important that you are not "ummm-ing" your way through the first part of the conversation. Coming in unprepared diminishes both your professionalism and the focus on finding a solution that will ultimately benefit the students.

Sometimes, knowing how to begin the conversation is the hardest part. Rehearsing a clear opening is key to whether the conversation becomes productive, or gets derailed before it even begins.

Consider practicing the following lines to open up the conversation:

"I'd like to talk to you about (name the problem in one sentence). You don't have to agree with everything I say, but I do ask you to please listen first."

"I've really been thrown off by a few things that I've seen (or heard), and I wanted to take this opportunity to address them."

Step 5: Be specific Whenever possible, avoid making general, "blanket" statements about an issue. Rather, use specific examples.

Was the colleague 12 minutes late to the meeting yesterday? Tell him, specifically, about the 12 minutes. Did the colleague say something offensive in the staff lounge? Quote specifically what she said. Only when we are willing to confront someone with specifics can the specific behavior be addressed and improved.

In addition, it is imperative that we separate behavior from self-worth. Telling someone that he came to the meeting late (behavior) is far more productive than telling him that he never gets anywhere on time (self-worth).

Step 6: Be real and listen. As Susan Scott writes in her best-selling book, *Fierce Conversations*, "Authenticity is not something you have; it is something you choose."

It's OK to laugh, to cry or to admit to being confused during a conversation. It's also OK if the conversation goes silent for a few moments. By bringing our authentic selves into a conversation, it enables us to lean *into* a conflict, instead of shying away from it.

Confronting a colleague does not mean that you do all the talking. Actually, after you have opened the conversation with your specifics, the majority of what you should be doing is *listening*. Listen to understand your colleague's perspective with a goal of finding solutions. Avoid fabricating your responses from the moment she opens her mouth (this is not listening!).

However, this doesn't mean letting your colleague turn you into a "dumping ground" for his issues and problems either. Part of being real is knowing your healthy boundaries, and when a conversation is not going well.

Should the conversation begin to go badly, or in circles, feel free to pause the conversation, and commit to coming back to the issue later. If necessary, tell your colleague that you feel the conversation is not going well, and that you feel your next step should be to call in an administrator or mediator.

Step 7: Make a plan. Conclude the conversation by agreeing on a plan of action, including how you will hold each other accountable. Too often, great meetings are concluded with everyone feeling better, but with no plan in place. This greatly increases the chances of the problem occurring again.

Simply saying, "So, what's the plan?" will move the conversation toward implementable solutions that will propel the cause forward. Once a plan is decided, make it official by *writing it down.*

Step 8: Appreciate and follow up. In the days and weeks after the conversation has ended, be sure to let your colleague know how much you appreciate working with her. Follow up on your action plan. Depending on the nature of the conversation, consider asking your colleague how she is feeling, or if she has had any further thoughts since you concluded.

You will have to use your professional judgment to decide how often and to what degree to bring up the issue. The greatest indication of how successful the conversation was is whether the conflict is ultimately resolved, and everyone involved is able to productively move forward.

IT'S UP TO US

Our students are counting on us to be at our best each day. To do this, we need to proactively and professionally handle the conflicts that inevitably arise when human beings work together.

If we see our own workplace conflicts as natural, and as opportunities for growth, we can address them calmly and positively. This helps our teams, and our schools, best serve the students who need us.

19

COMMUNITY-BASED PROFESSIONAL DEVELOPMENT

SIX STEPS FOR GETTING TEACHERS INTO THE COMMUNITY, AND THE COMMUNITY INTO TEACHERS

Last year, a visit to the Apple computer store led me to realize why Apple has, over the past 10 years, become the most progressive and powerful company in the world — while our schools have remained relatively stagnant in how we operate.

Scene One:

As I walked through the Apple store, I saw people sitting together at long tables, talking, playing with the latest techie products, and asking questions in a non-threatening atmosphere. Some left with new goodies, some left with their current gadget fixed or upgraded, and some left empty-handed after checking out items with interest. I felt a buzz of energy, curiosity and camaraderie among shoppers and staff.

Scene Two:

The next day, I went to a 3-hour professional development for teachers. We were crammed into a drab a room that was too small for the number of teachers there, we listened to a trainer who lectured at us, and we weren't given a break until one of the teachers in attendance spoke up and asked for it. In addition, we were all told <u>exactly</u> what we were expected to do when we returned to our classrooms the next day. There was barely any participation or connection. I felt a vibe of frustration, boredom, stagnancy and isolation within the stuffy, crowded room.

135

A week later, I bumped into a colleague who was also at that training, and asked if she had implemented the changes. "No," she said. "I was actually so uncomfortable that I couldn't really pay attention, and I found it hard to concentrate." As we walked off, I noticed that we were both busily looking at our iPhone screens. My mind flashed back to the excited atmosphere of learning that I had witnessed at the Apple store a week earlier.

Then, it hit me: *how could we make the atmosphere of our professional development meetings feel more like the Apple store?*

I saw it clearly: it was time for a change of scenery, a new environment and approach, to give our professional development a shot of energy, curiosity and camaraderie. We needed to get out of the dreary staff room and connect in new places and ways.

I've always been an advocate of neighborhood-based field trips with students to help connect us teachers with our students' communities. The Apple store/crowded training room dichotomy I had hit upon led me to look into educational "field trips" for teachers as well — to both connect us further with our students' communities, and to give a shot of energy to our staff professional development.

There is actually a formal name for this: it's called "Community-Based Professional Development" (CBPD). Our school district begun implementing CBPD this year, and so far, it has been a smashing success!

WHAT IS CBPD?

Community-Based Professional Development is professional development that occurs within the community that serves the students we teach. The main goal is simple: foster a stronger bond between the teachers who teach in a community, and the public who lives in that community.

The secondary goal is more subtle, but also important: to bring new life and perspective into often-dull professional development trainings for teachers.

CBPD can be held in a library, at a coffee shop, or in a restaurant — anywhere that teachers can get out from the traditional walls of their classroom or district conference room, and get into the community they serve (unfortunately, standing in a parking lot for 20 minutes discussing a teaching strategy doesn't count!).

Likewise, the public gets to see teachers in action: planning, collaborating and working hard to ensure the success of our students, who also happen to be their children.

In our district, we've found CBPD relatively easy to implement, and it has brought new life to both professional development for our staff and to our schools' connections in their communities.

SIX STEPS TO PLANNING A COMMUNITY-BASED PROFESSIONAL DEVELOPMENT

Here are some easy steps to make this happen in your school or district.

1. **Select a topic and a presenter.** While many professional development opportunities include bringing in a presenter, or expert, the point of CBPD is not to bring outside experts in; rather, to bring *inside experts out*. Pick a topic teachers would like to learn about, and find someone from within the school or district who would be willing to put together a workshop. Or, find someone who is willing and able to present in a compelling way, and have them select a topic they would most like to present on.

2. **Find a location.** It doesn't have to be anywhere fancy or hip. Check to see if the local library has a spare room. Or, remember that the typical time of afternoon that teachers finish their teaching for the day happens to be the exact time that restaurants and coffee shops are at their slowest point of the day (in between the lunch and dinner crowds).

At Your School

Ask them if they would be willing to let you use their banquet room, or section off a portion of their space for the teachers to gather. Remind them that the teachers will be purchasing coffee, drinks or food, and that they will most likely return with their families and tell others about the great experience they had there.

Many coffeehouse/restaurant owners have been in the community for a long time, probably went to school in the community where you now teach, and will be happy to help. This gives them a chance to support teachers and schools without having to make a straight donation. Of course, if they are willing to donate any food or drinks, that will only get teachers more excited about the event!

3. **Publicize it as an *experience*, not as a workshop.** Put in the time and effort to create a good-looking flyer, and get it to all of the teachers who might be interested. Explain that this is a fresh way to experience professional learning and connecting with each other and the community.

   Including details such as "Space is limited to 20 participants" will encourage teachers to register as quickly as possible. Of course, teachers love food, especially free food — make sure to let them know if food will be provided or available!

4. **Plan ahead.** Of course, the drawback to breaking away from the traditional locations is that you may be challenged to find an Internet connection or the necessary supplies. Be sure to secure all of the necessary supplies in advance, as well as a plan for getting them to the location and how they will be used once there.

   A restaurant owner might not be happy with you hanging things on the wall without advance notice, so check first. If you're planning to have food, but the establishment doesn't normally allow food, respect that and work with what you can do.

5. **Remind everyone of the intent.** While the experience is happening, be upfront about what you hope to accomplish: high-quality professional development in a setting that is local, stimulating, and mutually beneficial to the teachers and community.

   Before you begin, invite the owner/manager to say a few words about the location, and the products or services that it offers. They will most likely really enjoy the opportunity to meet some of the teachers!

6. **Follow up and build community.** In addition to the obvious thank-you note to the establishment that hosts the event, consider sending them a photo of the teachers "in action."

   Also, encourage teachers to return to the establishment on their own, and to tell the staff there that they attended the CBPD event, and are returning because of it. Turn participating teachers into "location scouts" by encouraging them to let you know if they happen to be somewhere that might make a good location for another CBPD.

   After the event ends, build upon it by creating a learning community that encourages the teachers who participated to stay in touch with each other. Provide opportunities for them to meet each other while the event is happening, including nametags or small group or partner discussions. Start an email list or a Facebook page to which participants can return to share ideas, ask questions, or think beyond the one event.

As you begin to implement Community-Based Professional Development, remember to get creative and dream big! Recently, our district's history teachers held an event in our city's Museum of History; teachers interested in learning about "Pinterest for Educators" met in the private room of a newly opened café; and a group of our physical education teachers were treated to a day of learning at the stadium where our professional baseball team, the San Diego Padres, play.

Whatever you decide, just imagine the energy of the Apple computer store as you imagine your next professional development. The time has come to break free from the traditional, often stifling, ways and places that are used to provide professional development for teachers — and open up to new places and ways of relating.

Our communities, schools, staff, and students, ultimately benefit from CBPD.

20

TURN JOB SHARES INTO "WIN-WIN-WINS"

FIVE WAYS TO MAKE SHARED POSITIONS WORK FOR TEACHERS, STUDENTS AND ADMINISTRATORS

(co-authored with Megan Pincus Kajitani)*

Recently, in a meeting about some staff issues at a school site, the principal told me that after her first year leading the school's staff, she abolished all job shares.

According to this principal, job shares — or the agreement between two teachers to share one contracted teaching position by coming in on different days — were ineffective, confusing for the students, and did not promote the highest levels of student learning.

She stated that it is her duty to ensure the learning of all students, which includes making "tough decisions," such as the one to disallow job shares at her site. Job shares, she said, are "great for the two teachers, but bad for their students."

As I left the meeting, I couldn't help thinking that while this decision might make things seem easier in the short-term, or even boost test scores for a year or two, overall, it hurts our society.

First, it forces working mothers (who occupy most job shares) into an "all-or-nothing" decision regarding choosing between mothering full-time or teaching full-time (same holds true for fathers). Second, it stifles the kind of creative thinking, relationship-building and flexibility that we *all* need to learn

141

(adults *and* youth) to thrive in the workplace of the future.

I kept asking myself: *Isn't there a way we can offer the flexibility of job shares to teachers and have students succeed at the same time? Aren't there job shares that work? And, what will it take to find a win–win here?*

So, I decided to do a little research, speaking with job-sharing teachers around our school district about what was working for them, and what was not. I also talked with principals about what they saw.

After identifying the pitfalls that "ineffective" job shares seem to fall victim to, I also pinpointed cases in which the job shares were "working," as demonstrated by the quantitative data. From these conversations, I came up with some concrete ideas for creating a win-win for teachers and students — *and* a win for administrators as well.

making JOB SHares WORK FOR everyone

Below are five strategies for creating and maintaining effective job shares that will allow *teachers* the work-life balance they deserve, *students* the high level of achievement that they are entitled to, and *administrators* a smoother ride in managing job share teams:

1. **Plan in advance.** Most teachers return to work the week before the students begin their first day in the Fall. Getting the room ready, attending meetings, making copies, and prepping Week 1 activities are usually the norm. However, for two teachers who will share a classroom and the same students, the regular prep week prior to school starting is too late to be shaking hands with your partner for the first time.

   Effective job shares are planned *the school year prior*, and this gives the participating teachers time to get used to each other and plan ahead.

When possible, each teacher should go and observe their soon-to-be partner in action in their classroom. Get to know your partner's teaching style, communication style, educational philosophy and supply closet!

Sit down and set some goals together, brainstorm ideas or create a job share mission statement. Then divide up some "homework" (to address the questions in tip #4, for example) and make some planning dates during Summer, so you as a duo can arrive in the Fall feeling dynamic, comfortable with one another, and prepared.

2. **Drop the attitude.** A teaching partnership is much more than the merging of two personalities (though that is a piece of it!) — it is the merging of two sets of supplies, two sets of expertise, and two sets of prior experiences. It is highly likely that both teachers come in with similar grade level and subject matter experience.

   Job shares that work are between two teachers who choose to drop the egos, scrap any thoughts of competition, and agree to cooperate, support one another, and encourage each teacher's success as individuals, and success as a team — which ultimately means student success.

As we often ask of our students, insist on being a lifelong learner. Be forthright regarding the strengths and weaknesses that you are bringing into the partnership. Your partner's weakness is yours as well, so look for solutions that will help you both, and that ultimately benefit the students.

The goal is to "adapt and adopt," rather than "outperform" your partner teacher. When one of you wins, you both win, and students win — same goes for losing.

In addition, take cues from your students about areas in which you can improve as a team. When a student says,

"Ms. X doesn't do it that way," this is a perfect chance to identify areas in which both teachers are not effectively communicating.

When a student says this, don't assign blame on your partner teacher; rather, see it as a normal part of this kind of arrangement — and an opportunity to improve your duo's communication and work cooperatively together to find solutions. Think of the example this sets for students about effective partnership and leadership in the process.

3. **Begin and end the year together.** On the first day of school, it is crucial that both teachers be present in the classroom. This gives the students the important message that there is no "one teacher" that is really in charge (even if one will be there more days). Present the situation as a benefit to the students, by explaining to them that they are members of only a few classes (or the only class) that get to have two teachers!

In addition, spend some time on the first day explaining to the students *why* you have both chosen to participate in this job share. It is important for our students to see that adults — especially the well-educated adults that we desire them to one day be — have work options, take those work options seriously, and are capable of prioritizing their own children as well as the students that they teach.

Be sure to explain to the students how you will be communicating with each other throughout the school year.

Along with the obvious methods of phone calls, emails and texting, show them the journal that you will be leaving for each other, as well as what you'll be communicating about. An effective journal will include student and parent updates, assignments due, unfinished work, etc. Perhaps you will also introduce a class website together, where both teachers will interact with students and parents.

Just as you begin the first day of school together, it is equally important to finish the last day of school together.

This sends a clear message to your students that you continue to care deeply for them all the way through to the end. It also sends a message about what teamwork means — and it's an excellent opportunity to make contact with their parents, many of whom show up on the last day of school to say goodbye.

4. **Put it in writing.** Let's be honest — sometimes the day-to-day grind of being a teacher results in us loosening our grip a bit on the procedures and routines that make our classrooms function smoothly. While this is understandable, with job shares, this poses a particular challenge, especially when one teacher holds to the routines and the other one doesn't.

This is why job share partners must work extra hard at setting and keeping consistent classroom procedures throughout the school year. Pull out that copy of Dr. Harry K. Wong's *The First Days of School* from your credential program and read it in tandem as soon as you sign your job share agreement in the Spring. As job sharers, it is critical that you put these kinds of procedures in place from Day One, and put them in writing.

Visibly posting the classroom procedures, routines and expectations, and training the students to recognize that what is posted is the "law of the land" can help avoid the uncertainty that can often occur. In addition, create checklists, or a handbook that includes what each teacher will agree to do during the day, at the end of each day, and/or the day before the other partner teacher's designated day(s) begin.

A teacher should never walk into the classroom wondering

what it will look like, or where something is. Moreover, avoid leaving your partner teacher "a pile of stuff" to deal with, instead of the opportunity to begin her day(s) with a clean lesson plan.

Finally, get down to the nitty-gritty. *How will work be displayed throughout the classroom? How will homework papers be formatted? What exact words and phrases will be used to discipline and reward students?* Showing solidarity is often the result of doing lots of little things the same way.

Of course you will adjust as you learn, but aiming for consistency from the start will only help you. It will be well worth paying attention to these details when you have two contented job share partners and successful, secure students.

5. **Set (flexible) limits.** Remember, for many, the goal of a job share is to balance the high demands of being a parent *and* a teacher. All too often, this results in a parent who spends too much time thinking about what is happening in the classroom, and a teacher who feels guilty for not being at home.

Acknowledge this, and work to find balance and boundaries together. Set limits on how often you'll talk, email and/or text — knowing these limits are for the benefit of everyone.

Yes, there are times when instant and frequent communication is critical; however, resist the urge to be in constant contact. I've seen job-sharing teachers texting their partners during their entire lunch period, which is a recipe for double burnout.

While having both teachers attend events such as Back-to-School Night or certain performances shows solidarity, it is not always necessary for both teachers to attend everything together. A successful job-share team I interviewed actually staggered their parent conferences in separate areas of the classroom, so both were visible but they met with parents separately. Be strategic in your planning!

Of course, there are times when flexibility is key to uphold consistency for students. For example, if one teacher knows she is going to be out sick or attending a training, it would be much more effective to have the partner teacher in the classroom on that particular day, instead of calling in a substitute teacher. Consider "trading" days in order to keep the students on the path of truly effective learning.

Studies show that part-time jobs can often bleed into full-time (which defeats the purpose, of course) — but it is possible to set healthy limits to keep both job share partners feeling their best, and thus teaching from their best.

MORE WORK, LESS WORK, WHATEVER WORKS!

Let's be realistic, when principals like the one I spoke with (who banned job shares) are suspect of the positive potential of this workplace practice, it is up to job sharers to go the extra mile to show how effective job shares can be.

Yes, as a part-time job sharer, you may have to plan ahead more, communicate more, and decide things in advance more than a typical full-time classroom teacher, but isn't it worth it for the flexibility?

The extra advance work will benefit you and the students in the long run, creating more security in the classroom environment for all, which we know leads to better student performance — and less work as the year progresses when your systems are running smoothly.

There may be a time in the near future when as many men as women are sharing jobs more, and sharing parenting more, which I bet many of you would applaud. To make this happen for all of us, though, we need to put in the time and effort now to make job shares cooperative for teachers, low-hassle for administrators, and effective for student learning.

Win-win-win job shares *are* possible, with proper planning and communication, and I challenge every school district to rise to the occasion and show our students this positive example of work-life balance and teacher teamwork!

**Special thanks to the job-sharing teachers in the Escondido Union School District who contributed their wisdom to this article, especially Mrs. Jennifer Byers and Mrs. Jenny Rhoades, whose expertise and experience are making a positive impact on the students they teach every single day!

*Megan Pincus Kajitani, M.A., is a professional writer, educator, and a former university career counselor and career columnist for The Chronicle of Higher Education and Inside Higher Ed. She left her full-time university position after having her first child, when her department head refused her job share proposal, and all job shares across the board. She is happy to have the opportunity to advocate for win-win-win job shares in education today.

PART THREE

TEACHER AS PUBLIC PROFESSIONAL

*Strategies for Making
a Positive Impact Beyond
Your School and Classroom*

21

THE GENERAL PUBLIC, ON TEACHERS

FIVE EASY WAYS TO HELP TURN OUR GREATEST FOE INTO OUR GREATEST ASSET

Recently, I was pushing my daughter on the swing at our local park. As happens often, the dad pushing the swing next to me and I began chatting, and eventually, talk turned to our jobs.

As soon as I said that I am a teacher, the conversation turned immediately to the popular headlines. Yes, he had just seen *Waiting for Superman*, and was now convinced that the teacher unions are to blame for our country's education woes — along with bad teachers and tenure.

Suddenly, I became the spokesperson for all bad teachers, all union decisions, and a system that awards tenure too easily. Sigh.

As teachers, we are often too busy, and too engaged in helping our students succeed, to stop and pay attention to the headlines. We are often too preoccupied to stop and defend the teaching profession to those who consider themselves experts on schools because they attended them as kids.

As a profession, we often lack the resources and training to "fight back" when we are lambasted in the media, by our politicians, or even on the playground.

Remember when Oprah badmouthed beef-eating on her show? The cattle farmers defended themselves vigorously, taking out full-page ads in major newspapers, taking her to court, and

Throughout Your Community

even managing to land themselves on many a late-night talk show, making "Oprah jokes" as the general public laughed along.

Most people know very little about what really goes into cattle farming. The same is actually true of classroom teaching — especially teaching at-risk students.

It's time we prepared ourselves to "fight back" — and productively engage in conversations about our profession with people outside of it.

FIVE WAYS TO FIGHT THE STEREOTYPES

The following strategies can help you sway those naysayers in the general public — whether you are at a cocktail party or on a playground — by helping them get more informed about the realities of our profession, and realize that teaching is one of the most rigorous, most profound, and most important jobs in the world.

1. **Stop reading the news, and start creating it.** The next time you read an education-related story in your local newspaper or magazine, take notice of the author. Often, an email address will accompany the article, especially in the online version. Keep these addresses on file, and the next time your classroom, school or district is doing something "newsworthy," email or call, and let the reporter know!

    You can also call your local paper and ask who their education reporter is. Often, reporters are under contract to write ten or so stories per week, and they are looking for things to write about. Furthermore, the way the Internet and news works these days, small, local stories sometimes turn into statewide or even national news!

    A positive news story about the work we are doing also gives it a sense of legitimacy and importance that can help sway public opinion in our favor.

2. **Tell stories.** Not stories about your own childhood, but about the realities that our students and schools face each and every day.

   Recently, I told a friend about a student who, after our promotion ceremony on the last day of school, refused to leave early, insisting that he stay for lunch. After much prodding and questioning from me, he finally yelled, "I just want to eat lunch one more time before I go home all summer to nothing!"

   A few days later, my friend told me that he couldn't stop thinking about the story I had told him, and couldn't get the image of the hungry student out of his head. He also realized how difficult the job of teaching is, especially teaching kids who are starving.

   Teaching is so much more than academic content and test scores; however, this is something that is often forgotten by the general public — and real stories make real connections that can remind them.

3. **Offer your soapbox.** Back on the playground, I eventually had the chance to ask the dad pushing the other swing what *he* did for work. It turns out that he's a scientist. "That's incredible," I said. "You have to come in and speak to my students!"

   A month later, he was standing at the front of my classroom, nervously telling 32 eighth-graders how he spends each day. Of course, his visit to my classroom also included a tour of our campus, a lunch in our cafeteria, and a peek into the classrooms of some of our other teachers.

   When he left, he was no longer an outsider questioning the validity of what teachers do. He was now a passionate member of the school community, ready to vigorously defend the hard work that we as educators do each day.

4. **Look the part.** Let's be honest: would you feel comfortable taking advice from a doctor who walked into your appointment in jeans and a t-shirt? Would you let a lawyer defend you in similar dress? Would you buy a car from someone in shorts and flip-flops?

   As educators, many of us have attained incredibly high levels of education in order to do the jobs we do, and we have every right to consider ourselves professionals. We are appalled when someone implies that we don't work hard. Shouldn't we dress accordingly?

   Each and every day, we have an opportunity to show hundreds of students how a professional dresses, along with the barista in the coffee shop, and everyone else we come into contact with on our way to and from our "office."

   I believe this isn't just about surface image, but about professionalism and respect for what we do. If we want the community to respect us as professionals, we must remember that how we look creates a lasting impression in the minds of those we interact with.

5. **Brag equally.** I have to admit, I was distraught when a colleague of mine posted the following on her Facebook page:

   > "Slept 'til noon, hanging at the beach. I love being a teacher on spring break."

   What message does this send to our non-teacher friends and acquaintances?

   One of the biggest misperceptions of the teaching profession is that we get "summers off, vacations throughout the year, and only work 6-hour days." Have you heard the diatribes coming out of the mouths of news pundits and politicians about Wisconsin teachers being on "the gravy train"? (Thank you, Jon Stewart, for defending us.)

The last thing we need to do is give off the impression that any of these fallacies are true.

Now, I'm not advocating a gag order on sharing the benefits of the teaching profession. I'm just saying, think about the messages you are sending. And if you feel the need to write social media posts similar to my friend's above, consider also posting:

> "Graded papers 'til midnight. Woke up at 5 a.m. and finalized my lesson plan. Ready for my teaching day!"

Or how about:

> "Enjoyed my half-hour lunch. Spent 15-minutes helping a student, and 15 minutes eating, using the restroom, and making 50 copies."

Or maybe:

> "Had an INCREDIBLE discussion with my class today about ways we can use math to be great athletes."

> "Totally worth the six hours of lesson planning to see my students make the connection in class today between the Civil Rights Movement and the recent election."

With social media as the dominant form of communication for many of us these days, why not use it to proactively defend, and realistically portray, the profession we all love so much?

I look forward to the day when I see a commercial for the teaching profession during the Super Bowl, or the day when teachers stand alongside movie stars and professional athletes as some of our country's most visible personalities.

However, until then, it is up to us as educators to spread the word about the incredibly challenging, incredibly rewarding work we do with our students, when we're in the classroom and out of it.

And *that* is a concept worth "liking."

22

START SPREADIN' THE NEWS

STRATEGIES TO SHINE THE SPOTLIGHT ON YOUR SCHOOL

Last week, at the annual "Title 1 Meeting" for a low-performing school in our district, I happened to sit next to a parent who was clearly nervous. When I inquired, she told me she was upset because she thought the meeting meant the school was being taken over.

I quickly explained that Title 1 status is determined simply by the number of students receiving free and reduced-price lunch, that this was just an informational meeting, and her children's school is not currently at risk of being taken over. Then, she visibly relaxed.

That exchange got me thinking about how often the only news people hear about education is *negative* news, and how it is becoming standard to assume the worst, especially when it comes to our schools with large numbers of at-risk students.

As educator-leaders working to improve the lives and futures of all of our students, I firmly believe it is part of our larger responsibility to communicate what is really happening in our schools, clearly and broadly, to parents and the larger community.

We are the marketing department!

I know… as teachers, we're busy doing what we're supposed to be doing: *teaching*. We are not taught in our credential programs to be public relations experts or marketing directors.

But, the truth is, if we don't become more savvy communicators with our schools' parents and communities, we actually miss an opportunity to better serve our students.

Clear communication with parents gives students a better chance of success, because if their caretakers feel connected with their school, students are more likely to get some support at home. And positive "press" elevates the morale of everyone at a school, and can be a great validating and motivating force for students who may need more encouragement about their work and potential.

True, many of our districts have a marketing professional on staff, and while they can be helpful (see below), they usually have more-than-full plates and focus on more regional communications.

So, the ball falls in our court to spread the news to our neighborhood parents and other citizens about the incredible work we're doing in our classrooms, the progress our school and students are making, and the importance of partnership opportunities that exist between a school site and the community that surrounds it.

So, how can we do that? It doesn't actually take much time and money, especially if a school staff team comes together to work toward the vision of clearer and broader communication with the larger school community.

FIVE TIPS FOR GETTING THE WORD OUT

Below are five low-cost ways that your school can begin to market itself, and start "spreadin' the news" about what's happening at your school site:

1. **Offer campus tours.** Led by someone who is well-versed in the school's mission, vision and inner-workings, campus tours offer parents of prospective students, community members, and local business members a glimpse into what is happening at a school.

They get to witness students and teachers hard at work, get a glimpse of curriculum as it is being taught, and ask relevant questions. If your school has something that it is especially proud of, such as interactive white boards, or an accomplished program, make sure the tour includes these "sightings."

Invite local business groups, Rotary Clubs, Chambers of Commerce, non-profits; advertise at the local libraries or in the local newspaper. Even offering a tour once a month can impact your school by bringing community members in to connect with the school, see what's really happening there, and feel a stake in its success.

2. **Create a high-quality website.** A high-quality website does not necessarily mean a high-cost website. With free websites available on sites such as Google or Wordpress, any fairly tech-literate person can now create a snazzy site that offers students, teachers and parents the opportunity to stay current on everything from school events to nightly homework.

   Chances are, there is at least one professional on your campus who could take on website design and maintenance, perhaps as their adjunct duty.

   Just as businesses rely on their website to connect with customers, provide relevant information, and communicate with its clientele, schools can do the same. Make sure to create a reason for people to go to the website, such as to gain necessary information regarding an upcoming event, or to check students' grades or teachers' blogs about their classes.

3. **Find your niche, and brand it.** My last school had an amazing video production program, where at-risk students produced award-winning short films. Another

school in the district has a phenomenal iPod reading program. Yet another has an incredibly effective, forward-thinking principal, with a clear mission.

What stands out at your school? Do people know about it? Think about what makes your school unique, in a positive way, and "brand" your school with these features and qualities.

If this is not immediately clear, you can come together as a staff and create a mission statement and/or tagline, and brainstorm ideas on how to make sure the community knows about what your school stands for. Pinpoint key players from your staff who can get out into the community and speak, and find opportunities for them to spread the message you want to send about your school and who you are.

4. **Use the news.** News outlets love a positive education story to fill the cracks between the negative news pieces, especially these days. Remember this, and start thinking about what is happening at your school that could make a good news story.

I have hooked newspeople into doing stories on grants our school received, awards students received, special field trips and campus guests. On that note, make your own news by inviting (or having students invite) high-profile visitors to your school site. Politicians quickly come to mind, but it is amazing how many high-profile people in other fields (arts, science, technology, publishing, academia) are also willing to help make a positive impact on students — don't be afraid to ask!

Have at least one person on your staff make contact with your district's marketing person, if you have one, and discuss the kinds of stories s/he looks for to feed to local news contacts. In addition, you can get to know the local education reporters yourself by emailing them about a story they have written or produced, or by sending them a story idea (such as the high-profile guest coming to your school next week!).

My wife is a former newspaper reporter, and she always reminds me that she had to come up with 10 stories a week, so she always appreciated a nice story being handed to her — remember this if you think reporters don't want to hear from you!

5. **Empower student voices.** The most powerful examples of our schools are, of course, our students themselves. Think about ways to empower them to share their successes and ideas, while practicing their communication skills at the same time.

An after-school journalism club could create a simple newsletter for parents and community members, with stories written by students (which parents may be more likely to read than a newsletter from the school's adults).

Here, I imagine how a student newsletter with a brief piece describing the Title 1 meeting would've helped the mother I met feel less intimidated — and give students an opportunity to really start talking about the issues in their community.

Over the years, I had many members of the media visit my classroom, and my at-risk students always rose to the occasion. Prepping them for reporters who might ask them questions always gave me perfect opportunities to coach them on the crucial skills of public speaking and interpersonal communication.

I also was sure to talk to them about *why* we wanted to make a positive impression to the media: to show the world that their neighborhood was not a negative place, but one full of amazing people like them who have so much to offer the world.

Yes, marketing your school can be seen as "not your job," or just "one more thing" to add to your busy schedule, and I know it is easy to be cynical about public relations, the media and all that.

But, think of the misinformed mother at the Title 1 meeting, the student whose eyes light up (and self-esteem skyrockets) when he sees himself featured in a local news story, and the potential partnerships and support those campus-touring Rotary Club members can offer to your school.

We can find real value in taking the time to work on this kind of intentionally positive communication as part of our role as a teacher-leader, who sees the bigger picture beyond the classroom.

23

Teaching Teachers

HOW TO STEP UP AND SHARE YOUR IDEAS WITH FELLOW EDUCATORS

There are thousands of books, experts and philosophies out there that tell us how to teach our students. But I truly believe that we teachers learn, implement and assess the strategies that work best by turning to *each other*.

As classroom teachers, we know that what works with one student might not work with another, and what works on Monday might bomb on Friday. But as we teach, day after day, and year after year, we've all found that within our successes are *strategies, tips and advice that work*.

MAKING IT OFFICIAL

Just as it's our responsibility as teachers to do everything we can to ensure that our students learn, it's also our responsibility as professionals to share our ideas with other teachers, so that *their* students can benefit as well.

And I don't just mean the casual conversations that happen in staff lounges, hallways and school parking lots, as great as those are. I'm talking about stepping up to share what you know in more formal settings — places such as scheduled staff meetings, conferences, and professional development events.

Don't you have some experience or wisdom you can share more formally with fellow teachers? Have you thought about applying to present at a meeting or conference, but haven't taken the leap yet?

Besides being a service to fellow teachers, I've found that becoming a "teacher of teachers" can be a wonderful way to reinvigorate yourself professionally — remembering why you chose to teach, and how far you've come in doing it. Furthermore, if you find yourself thriving at it, you can advance to more and larger venues, and teaching teachers can even become that important second income stream many of us rely on to pay our bills.

To encourage you to "just do it" — and share with other teachers in a more "official" way the wisdom you've gained in your classroom, I want to share with you some step-by-step strategies to make it happen.

Whether you are presenting in your school's library during a staff meeting, or in a huge conference hall (or anywhere in between), there are two steps to an effective presentation for teachers: preparing *before* the conference or meeting, and presenting *at* the event.

STRATEGIES FOR GETTING YOURSELF ON THE AGENDA

First, let's talk about before the event — how to come up with what you can share, and how to find someone who wants you to share it. Four strategies to get the gig:

1. **Pick your topic.** Decide what you would like to present on. Sometimes, the decision is made easy when your principal notices you doing something well, and asks you to present. Regardless, if you're having trouble deciding, ask yourself the following questions:

    - What am I most passionate about in education?
    - What do I do well in my own classroom, on campus, or within my education community?
    - What have the other teachers consistently asked me to share with them over the years?

2. **Write your blurb.** Once you've identified your topic, turn it into a presentation or workshop by selecting a title, and writing a 200-word description of what you'll discuss. Some conferences will require a description with less words; you can modify as necessary. Picking a catchy title always helps bring attention and audience members to your workshop, or gets colleagues a bit more excited.

3. **Make your pitch.** Find a meeting or conference at which you would like to present. I highly recommend starting with a local conference in your area. Find out how to submit a presentation proposal (sometimes called an RFP, "Request for Proposal," or an abstract). Each conference has a committee that selects presenters, and usually has a window of time in which you can submit your proposal.

4. **Be easy.** If you are notified that your proposal has been accepted, be sure to submit all information the conference organizers request from you in a timely, organized and friendly manner. Remember: conference organizers are extremely busy and overwhelmed. Showing them you are easy to work with will solidify your reputation as a professional!

STRATEGIES FOR SUCCESS WHEN YOU'VE GOT THE GIG

If you follow those steps, I'm sure you'll be scheduled to speak to fellow teachers in no time. And once you're on the docket, it's time to focus on making a true impact at the event. Here are five strategies for succeeding with your presentation:

1. **Be prepared and flexible.** Be sure to determine and communicate what equipment you will need to deliver a smashing presentation. Sometimes, projectors, screens and chart paper will be provided. Sometimes, they will not. Know in advance what will (and will not) be provided, and make sure you are prepared for it to work (or not to work!). Always have a "low-tech" backup plan.

2. **Go early.** When possible, get to the conference or meeting with plenty of time to spare. Whenever possible, I like to take a peek at the room I'll be presenting in, so I can begin to get comfortable with the surroundings. If there is another presenter in the room at the time, I try to listen to them for a bit, noticing things like lighting, acoustics and seating arrangements.

3. **Learn by doing.** Pay attention during your presentation. What is going well? What needs to be improved? Did they laugh at your joke? The first conference presentation I ever gave, "Making Math Cool," is one that I still give today. However, each time I present it, I notice something that could be tweaked or reorganized to be better. These days, that presentation is a lot better than when I first gave it!

4. **Connect the dots.** Whenever possible, make connections to things you heard other conference speakers say, or the school goals. Tell stories about your students and/or experience that highlight the concepts you are speaking about.

5. **Have fun.** Wherever it is that you're presenting, soak it in and enjoy it. If you're presenting at your school, ask your colleagues for their thoughts and opinions, and when possible, involve them in activities. At conferences, sit in on other presentations, introduce yourself to the people you're sitting with, and eat lunch with people you've never met before. Take what you learn from others, and share it with colleagues back at school.

As teachers, we stand in front of our students each day and teach the compelling ideas and concepts that they need to learn. As educators, the time has come for more of us to step up and present to our colleagues throughout the profession what we know works to engage students in learning and achieving.

Our students, or schools, and our profession stand to benefit greatly.

24

THE 5-5-5 OF TEACHER BLOGS

5 REASONS BLOGS ARE IMPORTANT
5 BLOGS YOU SHOULD BE READING
5 STEPS TO START YOUR OWN BLOG

Recently, a colleague asked me what I thought about the President's priorities in the upcoming year's federal education budget request. "Uh…" I stumbled, as I had not yet read up on the details. "Well, uh, gonna be interesting to see what happens…" I eeked out, then immediately ran to my laptop for consultation.

A quick check of the Department of Education's website gave me all the facts, but what I really needed were the well-formed thoughts, opinions and dwellings of my fellow teachers. I turned immediately to some "blogs" written by teachers I highly respect. Within a few clicks, I found myself informed, opinionated and ready to speak on the issue.

Blogs, short for "weblogs," have quickly become a popular way to share information, advertise businesses and analyze topics that are important to us as teachers. No, they're not the balanced and well-researched news that is (supposedly) found in newspapers; however, they are an excellent way to obtain information and opinions, often written in an uncensored, raw and real fashion.

In this column, I turn to the work of five of our country's finest educational bloggers. It should be noted that all but one of these blogs are written by classroom teachers. With so many decisions being made at the legislative level these days, now more than ever it is important for teachers' voices to be both heard and shared.

5 Reasons Blogs are Important

Why follow teacher blogs? Here are five reasons:

1. **Inspiration.** As teachers, our job can, at times, be difficult and depressing. Reading the real experiences of others helps us to stay motivated, compare experiences, and put into perspective the daily challenges we all face.

2. **Insight.** Sometimes there are issues, such as the federal education budget request I mentioned earlier, that I just don't know too much about. Reading blogs not only helps me wade through an abundance of information, it often helps me form my own opinions, which in turn helps me articulate those thoughts to others. I often find myself saying, "Oh, that makes sense," or "I totally agree (or disagree) with that person" after reading some of the blogs I mention below.

3. **Dialogue.** Most blogs are equipped with a feature that allows you to respond to an author's post. Often, the author will respond back, as well other readers. Geographical distance, which once prevented us from interacting with those outside of our school districts, has become a thing of the past, and blogs open up dialogue among teachers everywhere, shattering former barriers. If you especially like a blogger, you can often subscribe to their blog, so each time something new is posted, you'll be immediately notified by email.

4. **Community.** Having a hard time connecting with other science teachers at your school site? Blogs allow you to connect with like-minded teachers from all over the country. Not sure what to do about that student who is chronically tardy? Chances are, someone's blogged about it.

Blogs allow you access to an instant community, regardless of how that community is defined.

5. **Professional Development.** Not sure how to use your interactive whiteboard? Need help teaching your students to add fractions with unlike denominators? Reading blogs is free and easy, and you can often find the information you need, without having to drive to, sit through, and then not use the information from that professional development seminar at the district office that your principal just sent you to (you know it's true!).

5 BLOGS YOU SHOULD BE READING

Ready to start reading? Here are five blogs (in no particular order) that offer fantastic, deep and real insight into the world of teaching. I know that there are thousands upon thousands of blog entries being written each day, so if you know of a not-to-be-missed teacher blog, be sure to email me so I can update my list!

1. **Nancy Flanagan:** *Stranger in a Strange Land*
   http://blogs.edweek.org/teachers/teacher_in_a_strange_land/

   Written by the 1993 Michigan Teacher of the Year and a 30-year veteran K-12 music teacher, Nancy Flanagan offers her sharp-eyed perspectives on the inconsistencies and inspirations, the incomprehensible, immoral and imaginative, in American education. While reading, I often find myself laughing out loud, clenching my jaw, or thinking, "Jeez, she says it so much better than I ever could."

   Often, I find myself back at work the next day, seeing firsthand *exactly what she was talking about.*

2. **Bill Ferriter:** *The Tempered Radical*
   http://blog.williamferriter.com

Throughout Your Community

Written by Bill Ferriter, a full time sixth grade teacher and Solution Tree author, The Tempered Radical has earned broad recognition for its irreverent takes on topics ranging from the role of media specialists in the public schoolhouse to the damage done to today's students by standardized testing programs.

With a commitment to sharing what he knows about 21st Century Learning and a determination to bridge the gap between policymakers and classroom teachers, Ferriter's work is at once practical and entertaining.

3. **Heather Wolpert-Gawron:** *Tween Teacher*
   http://tweenteacher.com/blog/

By day, she's a 7th & 8th grade language arts/speech and debate teacher, but at night, Heather Wolpert-Gawron becomes "Tweenteacher," blogging the latest news in educational policy, curriculum design, and more importantly, how to more deeply enjoy this crazy and difficult calling of ours. She is always pushing us to continue to develop, or reignite, our love for teaching, with all of its obstacles and insults, and ultimately focus on developing our students' love of learning.

Tweenteacher is meant to help new educators, veterans, and second-career teachers navigate through this difficult yet rewarding career. It is also meant to challenge the past practices in our schools that do not work, while highlighting those that do.

4. **Tony Mullen: Road Diaries:** *2009 Teacher of the Year*
   http://blogs.edweek.org/teachers/teacher_of_the_year/

Beautifully written, this blog by Tony Mullen, the 2009 National Teacher of the Year (and a former New York City police officer-turned alternative high school teacher in Connecticut) chronicled his journeys as the country's 59th

National Teacher of the Year. His blog, like his travels, is a collection of esoteric thoughts and observations written for and about teachers.

Tony calls it like he sees it, often expressing frustration with a system that does little to support teachers in reality. In his blog entries, he often puts into words the universal feelings of all teachers. According to Tony, teachers are the fulcrum that supports this whole enterprise we call education, and people should be aware that any movement in that fulcrum affects us all. While all posts on this blog are now written "in the past," I find them to be universal and timeless as a teacher.

5. **Rick Hess:** *Straight Up*
   http://blogs.edweek.org/edweek/rick_hess_straight_up/

In his "Rick Hess Straight Up" blog at *Education Week*, the Director of Education Policy Studies at the Washington D.C.-based American Enterprise Institute think tank offers straight talk on matters of policy, politics, research, and reform.

Hess, a former high school teacher, influential author, and occasional college professor, brings an acerbic, national perspective to issues like governance, teacher evaluation, the use of evidence, and the Common Core. He's never warm and fuzzy, and some practitioners can sometimes find him infuriating, but he writes with a measured, hard-headed tone that makes his voice pretty distinctive and influential in national policy debates.

5 STEPS TO START YOUR OWN BLOG

Got something to say to the world about teaching? Interested in starting your own blog? Here are five ways to begin establishing your own platform for dialogue and change!

1. **Pick a Name:** The more intriguing the better, but pick something that can act as a unifying theme for your blog entries.

2. **Pick a Portal:** Blog portals such as WordPress and Blogger are leaders, and make it very easy to get started. There are others good options as well — just ask (or Google) around!

3. **Build your readership base.** Usually, telling your friends, family and colleagues is enough to get started. Share your blog with your Facebook contacts. Be sure to tell them to recommend your blog to others!

4. **Find other bloggers, and link up!** Most blogs allow you to feature other peoples' blogs on your site. In return, other bloggers will link your site to theirs.

5. **Go beyond words.** The written word is great, but consider including pictures, music, videos, coupons, and other items of interest on your blog. In this age of multimedia, going beyond just writing will help keep your blog fresh, entertaining, and give your readers a reason to come back for more!

There are a lot of people who have something to say about teachers and the state of education these days. But are they teachers? Not enough of them.

Whether you're using blogs to gather information, speak your mind, or champion a cause, this modern form of communication offers a chance to let your teacher voice be heard widely. Happy blogging!

WHY ARE SO MANY KIDS FAILING MATH?

HOW ALL TEACHERS CAN COMBAT MATHEMATICAL ILLITERACY, INSIDE AND OUTSIDE OF CLASS

If you are a math teacher, like me, you know the conversation all too well. It usually goes something like this:

> **Them:** It's nice to meet you. What do you do for a living?
>
> **Me:** I'm a math teacher.
>
> **Them:** Oh, I hated math! Was never any good at it — so boring, and useless!
>
> **Me:** (slightly flustered) Well, um, how 'bout those Padres?

Most math teachers are tired of hearing about how awful people are at math, and many of us just don't want to deal with this typical response to our profession.

However, I've recently realized how this exact conversation can actually be a priceless opportunity to make a critical change in our nation's math crisis.

TIME TO STOP LETTING IT SLIDE

The above conversation reflects much more than one individual who couldn't compute the slope of a line, or recite the quadratic formula. It shows a *socially acceptable attitude* that it's OK to be bad at math, and to hate it.

Throughout Your Community

This is an attitude that we, as a culture, and as teachers, have allowed to persist, and even to grow.

Imagine telling someone that you "always hated reading, and were never good at it," and how relieved you are that you never have to read in your job. You would be pegged an illiterate.

However, mathematical illiteracy has become a casual joke in our society.

With 70 percent of our nation's 8th graders performing below proficient in mathematics, it is evident that we have a real cultural problem on our hands. This is no joke — it's a serious issue that teachers of any and all subjects need to face head-on.

As teachers, we possess the power and tools to begin turning this societal attitude about math around, both in and out of the classroom. We also possess the *obligation* to do so.

STUDENTS FIRST

Let's start in the classroom, where our impact is most direct. The two misnomers we so often hear outside of the classroom — that math is boring and that it is useless — are also repeated daily by students.

With a proactive attitude, a little creativity, and a healthy sense of humor, we can turn these myths around for students. Here are some ideas to start with:

> **Misnomer #1: Math is boring.** Let's be honest here: in a world of iPods, social media, cell phones, and video games, math *is* boring. Sure, most of us teachers don't allow these particular tech devices in our classrooms. However, we are still in direct competition with them.
>
> Maybe it's not the actual math that bores the students — perhaps it's the way we are presenting it to them.

Why not, instead of battling these enemy pastimes, use them to our advantage? Bring the fast-paced world of the students into the classroom, and show them how each and every one of their technologies relies on a knowledge of math (so how boring can it be?).

Here are some strategies to do just that:

- Capitalize on students' love for video games and internet by using websites such as www.coolmath.com, www.mathplayground.com, and www.braingle.com that offer an alternative to the old pencil-and-paper routine.

- Use the students' world in your examples. Just the other day, when I related math shortcuts to texting abbreviations such as LOL and BRB, I suddenly had the rapt attention of my entire class.

- Did you know that almost every cell phone has a calculator feature? Imagine if after doing a math problem, you told your students to whip out their cell phones to check their work. Or, make up word problems about their usage minutes, and how to choose the best plan.

- There are math songs (like my math raps) on iTunes that students can download onto their iPods as assignments. Show them that their favorite musical gadget is yours, too, and you earn their respect and attention in the process.

Of course, allowing the students to use their cell phones or iPods in class requires proper front-loading of what is expected of them. But I've found that the students are so excited about sanctioned use of their toys that they don't abuse the privilege.

Misnomer #2: I'm never going to use this in my life. Many adults perpetuate this myth, even though they use math every day without knowing it.

As we teachers understand, even if they don't directly involve numbers, skills such as solving problems, exploring options, and staying organized are all math-related. It's our job to make sure the students understand this, too.

Strategies to shift their perspective:

- My best weapon to combat this misnomer: Don't teach alone. Show the students, through real people coming into your classroom, that every job uses math. A 15-minute visit is often enough to turn a student's light bulb on.

  Don't limit it to just doctors, lawyers, and accountants either. Bring in plumbers, construction workers, store clerks, and truck drivers. "Keep it real," as our students say, with people from their surrounding neighborhood (or at least represent their ethnicity and socioeconomic status), and shed the pocket-protector math geek image in the process.

- My other favorite activity in this vein is called "Stump the Math Professor." Students throw out absolutely any (classroom-appropriate) topic, and I (as Math Professor) tell them how it relates to math. Soccer? Scores, angles, speed. Pizza? Temperature, cooking time, slices. Get silly, have fun with it.

  Students constantly request this game, which I always back up with my rap called "Math is Everywhere." They often tell me that they, too, start to see math in places they never imagined.

In short, part of our teaching needs to be ingraining in students' consciousness the fact that math applies to their life every single day.

Arm them with this knowledge and they become part of our army out on the streets challenging those people who say math is useless. Culture changes one person at a time.

THE NEXT TIME...

Beyond the classroom, it comes back to that inevitable dinner party conversation. So, the next time someone tells me they "hated math," perhaps I'll say, "That's because we live in a society that has allowed mathematical illiteracy to flourish."

Or maybe I'll retort, "Funny, I just read an article about that statement," and spark the conversation about math misnomers, and why what we're saying outside of the classroom is fueling a crisis in our schools and our society.

ABOUT RAPSA

REACHING AT+PROMISE **STUDENTS®** ASSOCIATION

A portion of the profits from sales of this book go to RAPSA (The Reaching At-Promise Students Association).

RAPSA is a leading professional development and networking organization for those working with the at-promise student population, and has a membership of hundreds of educators internationally, including teachers, administrators, counselors, coaches, volunteers, and community members.

RAPSA's vision is to

- Empower all students to become contributing members of society.

- Support educators and community members by keeping them well informed with current practices and presenting them with a variety of proven teaching and intervention strategies.

- Work to improve educational outcomes for all students.

To learn more, visit www.rapsa.org.

ABOUT THE AUTHOR AND EDITOR

Alex Kajitani and Megan Pincus Kajitani are the co-founders of Kajitani Education, which provides teacher education and lifestyle education, with the motto: *"educating for the world as it can be."* Together, Alex and Megan create books, trainings and online membership communities to inform and connect those who aspire to create a better world.

Alex Kajitani is the 2009 California Teacher of the Year, and a Top-4 Finalist for National Teacher of the Year. He is also known around the country as "The Rappin' Mathematician," and his CDs and activity books are being used in thousands of homes and classrooms, getting kids around the world excited about math! He speaks nationally on a variety of education issues, and delivers powerful keynote speeches and workshops to support and motivate teachers. His work has been praised by education leader Dr. Harry K. Wong (*The First Days of School*) as "some of the most creative work I've ever seen a teacher do."

Alex is also the author of *The Teacher of the Year Handbook: The Ultimate Guide to Making the Most of Your Teacher-Leader Role*, and has contributed to several education books, including *Conversations With America's Best Teachers* and *Chicken Soup for Soul: Teacher Tales*. He has been featured in many media stories, including *The CBS Evening News with Katie Couric*, and has delivered the popular TED Talk, "Making Math Cool." Visit www.AlexKajitani.com to learn more about Alex's work.

Megan Pincus Kajitani is a professional writer, editor and educator for over 17 years. She has written columns and essays for newspapers, magazines, books and online media outlets, including *The Chronicle of Higher Education*, *The Huffington Post*, *Inside Higher Ed*, *Mothering Magazine*, and others. She has served as an editor for many books, including the *New York Times* Bestseller, *The Daring Book for Girls*.

Megan has a Master's degree in Media & Cultural Studies from the University of Wisconsin-Madison, and completed Ph.D. coursework and a Certificate in Training & Career Development at the University of California-San Diego. She also trained in humane education and plant-based nutrition to launch her latest project, Giraffe Revolution. Learn more about Megan and her work at www.GiraffeRevolution.com.